This is Buenos Aires

Lily Benmayor

This is Buenos Aires

A sightseeing guide to the city

Ediciones
Arte y Turismo

Published by Ediciones Arte y Turismo
Av. Las Heras 3115, 12º "47" - Buenos Aires
Tel. 801-5657
Printed in Argentina
Legal deposit (Law 11.723) duly made
ISBN 950-43-2362-6

Cover design by Luis Perrone

This book is an abridged translation
of *Buenos Aires es así*, by Lily Benmayor
Other books by the same author:
Sea usted su propio guía (an artistic European tour)
Nuestro Teatro Colón

Contents

Preface

For much too long a time Buenos Aires has been deprived of a useful tourist guide. Accustomed to the travel facilities of more developed countries, a visitor on his first trip to the capital of Argentina must have felt ill-equipped for navigating such a wide spread and multifaceted city as ours.

This is the gap we wanted to bridge with the book we are presenting to our readers, well aware that it wasn't an easy task to satisfy the expectances of all English speaking tourists

Special care was taken not to turn this guide into an encyclopaedia. Buenos Aires, although a relatively young city, possesses enough history and geographical extension to fill more than one volume of information. However, it is our belief that a thoughtful selection of sights and facts will suit the tourist's purposes much better than an overcareful list of every single spot to be seen or known in the city.

We also tried to avoid an overly encomiastical approach to the matter; on the other hand, we didn't hesitate to unveil the defects which in our opinion can spoil the charm of our beloved "Reina del Plata".

But probably our largest obstacle was to tackle the never ending urban renewal of Buenos Aires. It is a fact that the city changes from day to day. What was here today might be gone tomorrow, where a great shopping center could be found stands now a piano bar, which in turn will soon become a theatre, a block of flats, or a green open area.

In other words, this was no small undertaking. But certainly worth the effort. Whether our intention has been accomplished or not, only our readers and time will tell. Meanwhile, let's hope this is the book Buenos Aires was waiting for, and the tourists from abroad fully deserved.

Some general information

- Buenos Aires, capital of the Argentine Republic, is a city/port situated on the right bank of the River Plate, at 34°37' south latitude.
- It spreads out over an area of 200 square kilometers and has a population of some 3,200,000, rising to 8 million including the outskirts (Gran Buenos Aires).
- The climate is warm and humid, with an annual average temperature of 17° C.
- *Porteño* is the name given to the native of Buenos Aires.
- Argentine currency is the Peso, divided into 100 cents. There are bills of 2, 5, 10, 20, 50 and 100 Pesos; and coins of 5, 10, 25, 50 cents and 1 Peso.
- Argentina's official language is Spanish. English, French and Italian are widely spoken or understood.

Entry requirements

- Citizens of neighboring countries (Uruguay, Brasil, Para-guay, Bolivia and Chile), need identity card.
- Citizens of other American countries: passport (not visaed).
- Citizens of West Germany, Austria, Belgium, Denmark, Spain, Finland, France, Greece, Holland, Ireland, Italy, Japan, Liechtenstein, Luxemburg, Norway, Portugal, Sweden and Switzerland: passport (not visaed).
- Citizens of other countries: passport, with consular visa. Validity of visa: 90 days.

To prevent any possible change in the regulations, tourists are recommended to check them out at Argentine consulates before travelling.

Non-working days in Argentina

January lst. (New Year)
Good Friday
May lst. (Workmen's Day)
May 25 (First Argentine Government)
June 10 (Malvinas Day)
June 20 (Flag Day)

July 9 (Independence Day)
August 17 (General San Martin's anniversary)
October 12 (Discovery of America)
December 25 (Christmas)

*Should you need additional information about Buenos
Aires, apply to the Municipality Information Centers.
You'll find them at Ezeiza and Jorge Newbery Airports,
and along Florida street.*

When to visit Buenos Aires

This is such a personal matter, that we had to think it over
before including it as practical information.

If your decision depends primarily on the climate, then **Autumn** is the perfect time. The trees still in bloom display their
wonderful multicolored foliage, the weather is stable and the
temperature, moderate. Moreover, this is the period when B.A.
returns to its normal activity after the summer rest, without
however reaching the frenzy of the winter months nor the cra-
zy comings and goings of the Christmas rush. And yet, autumn
has also its ups and downs. Rains can be quite persistent and
spoil the plans of the most optimistic of tourists.

Winter is also a most pleasant period, with plenty of sunny
days and mild temperatures which only require you to wear a
light overcoat. However, we do sometimes have to put up with
pretty cold mornings of one or two degrees, and even less if a
southerly wind is blowing; fortunately the sun sbines most of
the time and that mitigates the cold feeling.

If you are wondering whether it ever snowed in B.A., we have
to confess that it did, but only once and that was ages ago, back
in 1918, so we don't think it is likely to happen again.

Another whim of our v.inter season is the so-called Verani-
to de San Juan (Saint John's Little Summer), a most unusual
period lasting one or two weeks right in the middle of June,
when the thermometers rise to absurd levels and colds are a
dime a dozen.

Perhaps it would be wiser you bet on **Summer**. Mind you it
can get pretty warm, and uncomfortable too if you can't suffer

damp and low pressure days. In January, which is the hottest month of the year, you'll be experiencing an average 30°C, but you may also be forced to enjoy anywhere between 35 and 37°C. We actually hit a record of 43°C back in 1957, but it has so far never been that high again; on the contrary, the weather can be really pleasant during early evening and at night, especially if a fresh river breeze lends a hand.

Furthermore, summer has the advantage of a half empty city in which you will be able to easily ramble around, find bookings for any show, and even get a seat on the bus. But some theatres close down during this season, since they take their shows mainly to the seaside resort city of Mar del Plata. The same must be said of museums and other public places, as well as some shops and boutiques; to compensate, sales are at their best. Anyway, there is plenty to see and visit, so don't let what we have just said dishearten you.

As far as **Spring** is concerned, it usually comes in rather blustery, which however does not hamper the fact that B.A. likes to celebrate the coming of the flower season with much pomp and ceremony. On September 21st, crowds of porteños, all decked up in white and slightly blue with cold, turn out onto a gaily decorated Av. Santa Fe as though it were really warm. As a matter of fact, only in mid October, when everything is in full blossom, we finally realize that spring has sprung. But then, when the weather has settled, touring B.A. is simply glorious.

In short, Buenos Aires has a mild climate from January to December, with no temperatures reaching old extremes, radiant sunny days during most of the year, and a few meteorological surprises which however never become catastrophic.

That is why we would simply like to tell you: come when you are willing to, when you think it more convenient, whenever you feel like visiting Argentina. No doubt, that will be the best time for you to come to Buenos Aires.

What should be known

Buenos Aires was founded twice. Once by Pedro de Mendoza, in 1536. A poor and miserable settlement, besieged by indians, hunger and beasts, it did not take long for it to disappear. Fourty four years later, Juan de Garay had another try, this time for good. Commanding a handful of men, he came to shore in 1580 and on June 11th of that same year founded the Ciudad de la Trinidad y Puerto de los Buenos Ayres (City of the Trinity and Port of St. Mary of the Good Airs). Shortly after, Buenos Aires for everybody.

For almost two centuries, insignificant when compared to the powerful Peruvian Viceroyship, the city vegetated anonymously. And yet, under the colonial drowsiness, Buenos Aires was growing. Its port, cleverly exploited by the settlers, gave birth to an economic prosperity which, together with the urgent need to put an end to piracy in the region, induced the Spanish crown to raise the juridical status of the city. In consequence, in 1776 Buenos Aires was declared the capital of the newly created Viceroyship of the River Plate, quickly becoming the undisputed leader of the South American continent.

The British invasions of 1806 and 1807, successfully repelled by the porteños, hastened matters. Aware of their strength, spurred by the French ideas of freedom and equality, annoyed by the Spanish commercial monopoly to which they were submitted, the porteños felt the time had come for liberation. On May 25th 1810 a local government was created and six years later, on July 9th 1916, independence was declared.

The years that followed were by no means easy. Wars against the Spanish armies on one hand, a fratricide struggle with the provinces —not always keen to accept the ideals of May— on the other, gradually led to a generalized anarchy which disrupted the old territory of the Viceroyship and caused Buenos Aires to lose its traditional supremacy over the rest of the country.

And so, barring a brief period headed by President Rivadavia, the city as from 1820 was reduced to just another capital of a province rather than the principal seat of the Nation. Like the rest of the provinces, Buenos Aires suffered the ills of tyranny, backwardness and ignorance when in 1835 Rosas assumed power and handled the country's destiny according to his arbitrary whims.

In 1852, Urquiza put an end to Rosas dictatorship. but the conflicts with the rest of the country were yet to be solved and for another ten years B.A. lived as an independent state, separated from the provinces.

Finally, in 1862, the battle of Pavon sealed national unity and the city was able to return to the road it had set out in 1810. A road which led to an economic, cultural and social growth, thanks to many different factors.

First and foremost, capable and honest men, rulers such as Mitre, Sarmiento and Avellaneda, who put the country on the path of work and education; a very active port which filled both official and private coffers daily; and the most important factor of them all, a flexible mentality open to culture, progress and change.

Last but not least, the immigrants.

Packed in the promiscuity of the conventillos (tenement houses for several families), working from dawn till dusk, skimping, saving and studying rather than sleeping, those Italians, Spaniards, Jews, Sirian-Lebanese, and many others, who brought to the River Plate the virtues and sins proper to their communities as well as a determined ambition of progress, slowly changed the face of B.A. and developed a new type of porteño.

Struggles for power, class differences and integration problems were ever present. But in the long run, merged with the sons of the land and having become scientists, men of letters, statesmen, industrialists, artists and technicians, they contributed decisively to that which, in essence, is the real worth of Buenos Aires: its cosmopolitan spirit, its vocation for culture, its inmost attachment for democratic principles.

Between 1852 and 1930, the city grew at such a rate, that today it seems science-fiction.

A clever educational policy multiplied schools and universities; improvements in street lighting, generalized paving, and the development of the transport system brought the center closer to the suburbs, expanding B.A. until it became one of the largest cities in the world. Hospitals, markets, movie houses, theatres and the like supplied the needs of a population which, in the course of 80 years, had almost tripled in number. For that ever growing population public buildings were constructed, as well as living quarters for all social levels: from the luxurious French-styled palace to the humblest of brick houses, made by the workers themselves during their weekends.

Needless to say, not everything was idyllic nor was life a bed of roses, but confidence in one's own effort as well as a tremendous will to grow were common in everybody; there was tenacity, optimism and discipline, and the results were there for everyone to see.

This world suffered its first set back in 1930, when a military conspiracy altered the democratic order, opening the doors to an era still polemic, still painful, which in an overall manner can be divided into three periods.

Until 1943, the sweeping inertia of the previous period blanketed the dark ground of reality. Nothing apparently had changed. New avenues continued to be constructed, monuments were erected, the city became more beautiful and cultural life was at its best. However, under that superficial glitter, an economic crisis loomed which generated humiliation and resentment, preparing spirits for new and drastic transformations.

In 1943, power was again taken over by the military, who installed a regime which many viewed as the panacea to all ills. How true this was, only time and history will tell. The fact is that, from one crisis to another, B.A. sank into a political, economic and specially social chaos which did away with ethical rules and divided Argentines into two irreconcilable bands. The city felt the impact and changed its face for the second time on having to untidily adapt to a completely different standard of living. Freeways, great towering apartment buildings, huge supermarkets channeled the needs of an oversized human mass which in 1970 had already exceeded eight million souls.

The last period is still very much in the public eye and heart. Between 1973 and 1983, the hatred and frustrations accumulated during so many decades of latent war exploded with unusual violence on the side of both parties concerned, dragging the country into guerrilla warfare, repression, fear and, finally, indiscriminated genocide.

Today, the nightmare is over.

"The Founding of Buenos Aires by Juan de Garay"
This is how Jose Moreno Carbonero imagined the historical event.
The painting can be seen at the National Historical Museum.

Eating is also a must

If there is something easy in Buenos Aires is to find a nice place to eat.

The excellence of Argentine meat is of course a well known fact, but grills are not your only choice. Like any other cosmopolitan city in the world, B.A. can offer everything you can imagine, from French cuisine to kosher meals. As for pizza, we daresay porteños have beaten all the records, both as for quality and assortment.

Most common are the restaurants serving continental dishes, where you can have a juicy steak or an excellent pasta cacerole, *pulpo a la gallega* (octopus) or a wide variety of regional *empanadas* (small pastry wrap-overs filled with meat, or chicken, or cheese and ham, or corn, etc.).

A complete list of B.A.'s restaurants could probably fill more than one volume and so we'll only hint you on those typical, well known, or for some special reason standing out from the rest. Surely many houses will be left out and it is not improbable that by the time this book comes out, many will have closed down and new ones opened. We have grouped them into each sightseeing tour so that you can have all possible choices right in the area being visited, without any loss of time.

Now, if you are looking for fast foods or a quick snack, all you've got to do is to look right and left and go in. But beware, that isn't either an easy decision!

How to get around

Although our itineraries can and should be covered on foot, to reach every single area and move around through such an sprawling metropolis as B.A. requires an efficient transport system to make the task easier. Our city can boast a very good one.

The *colectivo* (small bus) service is excellent both as frequency and areas covered, so that the farthest corner in the city and its surroundings is easily reached by the 150 or more lines of the system. You purchase your ticket directly from the driver as you get on the bus, indicating where you want to go, since the price of the fare some times varies according to the distance you are going to travel. A bus stop sign every two blocks indicates the main route the service takes you along.

Another efficient means of transport is the *subterraneo* (subway). There are five lines, some of them intercommunicated. Interchange can be made at the following stations:

Independencia	Lines C and E
Carlos Pellegrini Diagonal Norte } .... 9 de Julio	Lines B, C and D
Lima } .... Av. de Mayo	Lines A and C

NB: You'll note that trains circulating through one-way stations keep to the left. This is because traffic in B.A. was long ago ruled by this code. The change to the right side was only decreed after the subway system was completed.

The subway is by far the quickest way to go around in any congested metropolis of the world, and B.A. unfortunately occupies a reputable although rather annoying privileged place among them. Its natural handicap, from the tourist's point of view, is well known: the passenger misses a great deal of the urban scenery, which is always so attractive for anybody touring a city for the first time.

As for the taxi (painted black and yellow), no doubt it is easy and comfortable, with no tickets to be bought, no searching for the right line, when to get down, etcetera.

Very comfortable, yes. But scarcely exciting for a tourist. That is why we suggest you leave the ease to the long suffering inhabitants of B.A. and travel, whenever you can, in our colectivo. It certainly will be a good way to get to know the city at a low cost and learn at the same time about the porteños' idiosyncracies and their complex personality.

Just pay careful attention to the driver and his polished academic maners towards the passengers; bravely put up with the squeeze during rush hours; do not become horror struck at the sudden jerks when starting or breaking, which are the characteristic driving style of these heroic servants of our community; let yourself be lulled by the screaming harmony of their audio equipments; enjoy the sweet smoky atmosphere of the vehicle in spite of the non-smoking warnings...

Oh well! Nobody is perfect!

And now, the sightseeing

It is very easy to grasp Buenos Aires' layout. Since it is a rather young city, it never acquired those puzzling concentric streets and winding little roads of the old medieval towns. On the contrary, right from its foundation, B.A. was built like a chess board, that is to say, with streets crossing each other at straight angles, forming manzanas (squares) whose surrounding streets we call cuadras (blocks).

The initial nucleus, a quadrilateral of 144 squares bordering the river, opened out like a fan, extending in the direction of the roads leading to the interior of the country

The road to the west, now Rivadavia Ave., is the backbone of Buenos Aires. Rivadavia is a tremendously long artery which crosses the whole city from east to west and divides it into two great zones: North and South. All streets perpendicular to it change their names according to which side of the dividing line they are on. Florida, for example, is the name of the street on the north side, but changes to Peru when entering the southern sector. Exceptions to this rule are Av. 9 de Julio and Av. Gral. Paz (a ringlike avenue that separates the city proper from the Greater B.A.), both maintaining their name throughout their full length.

With time, these routes to the interior became avenues and others were added, parallel to them at four blocks intervals between each other. Corrientes, Cordoba, and Santa Fe in the northern sector; Belgrano, Independencia, San Juan, and Caseros towards the south.

From east to west, this regularity is not so exact, but there still are avenues which every now and then put virtual limits between zones. The most important are Callao and 9 de Julio. Callao was the western boundary of the city when its first enlargement took place; today it practically separates the center from the inner districts. As for 9 de Julio, on reaching Constitucion Station it joins up with Montes de Oca, the ancient access to the southern zone, still in use.

Parallel to the river, a long avenue runs which changes its name according to the quarters it goes through. It is called Alm. Brown and Paseo Colon in the south, Leandro N. Alem and Av. del Libertador through the northern districts, the latter maintaining its name as it runs through the suburban localities which border the coast. Popular jargon has merged all these names into *el Bajo* (the Lower Road), in allusion to the lowlands adjacent to the river, as opposed to the table-land on which B.A. is built.

Different districts cropped up flanking the great avenues. Palermo and Barrio Norte have Santa Fe Av. as their axis; around Corrientes rose Villa Crespo, Chacarita and Villa Urquiza; dependent on Rivadavia are Once, Almagro, Caballito, Flores and Liniers. And a lot more which we do not really find it necessary to mention here. Poetically, they were all referred to as *Los Cien Barrios Porteños* (The 100 City Districts). Actually they are not that many but just a little under a half, which is still a pretty considerable number.

Generally speaking, it can be said that the elegant quarters are grouped on the northern zone, while the lower-classed ones are found in the south, differences becoming more noticeable according to their distance from Rivadavia: lavish luxury bordering Av. del Libertador, poverty and slums alongside the Riachuelo (a small tributary of the River Plate).

And here you have a practical piece of information that will help you keep your bearings: the number on the houses increases by the hundred after each block; odd numbers are always on the right of the street as the numbering rises, even numbers are therefore on the left. This is a golden rule for you to move around unbewildered the length and breadth of the city.

Tour I

Plaza San Martin
Retiro
Florida Street

There is no better way to start getting acquainted with Bue-nos Aires than a walk through the Plaza San Martin area.

Two important commercial thoroughfares, Av. Santa Fe and Florida St., branch out from here, displaying a wide variety of shops crowded by residents and tourists alike. Surrounding the park are some of the most representative buildings, palaces and hotels in the city. From its highest point, a splendid panoram-ic view of the area can be afforded, with a treed slope at your feet and the feverish bustle of Retiro Station across Libertador Ave., pouring over the city thousands of people in search of work, entertainment and companionship.

A little history

Wild and solitary was this area in its origin. People called it El Retiro (The Retreat) on account of a hermitage lying in the surroundings, while trustworthy documents state that Gover-nor Miguel de Riglos' summer house was constructed there.

In 1719, the man seems to have run into economic trouble and sells the property, later transformed into a slave market. It would take a century for the Cabildo to dislodge it, order its demolition, and replace it with a bull fighting arena. But that construction did not last long either. In 1819, bull fighting is forbidden in B.A. and the ring torn down.

In the meantime, Retiro had served as battle grounds dur-ing the British invasions (1806/07); military buildings were con-structed too, that would later house San Martin's famous grenadier regiment. The zone was then called Campo de Marte

(Camp of Mars) and only after the fall of Rosas did this warlike face start to change.

First, the monument to San Martin was erected. Then Sarmiento had the site turned into a park, which in its upper part was called Plaza San Martin after Argentina's national hero, the lower land retaining the old name of Retiro. The military barracks demolished, railway stations were constructed, avenues were opened, residences and hotels began to appear, until Plaza San Martin became one of the most important and beautiful areas in Buenos Aires.

PLAZA SAN MARTIN

The charm of this park is due mostly to its asymmetrical layout and diversity of levels, which is a rather unusual feature in a flat city like Buenos Aires.

A good starting point for your touring is the corner of Libertador Ave. and Juncal St. Winding uphill paths will lead you to the highest part of the park and a more than worthwhile panoramic view.

Plaza San Martin was designed by the French landscaper Carlos Thays. Aided by a humid climate in which both native

San Martin Park
The Pirelli Building on the right.

and exotic species could easily grow. Thays combined willows, linden trees, *jacarandas* of small blue flowers, palm trees, centenary hardwoods, rubber plants, our local *palo borracho* (drunken stick) with its funny belly-like trunk and its lovely pink flowers, silkwood, and a lot more, creating a gorgeous scenario for the surrounding buildings and the many pieces of sculpture scattered all over the greenery.

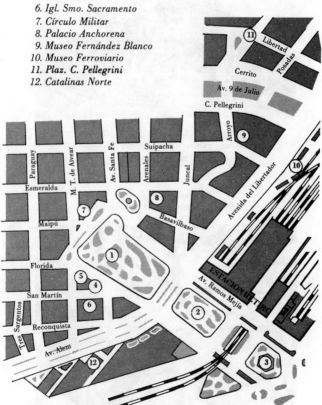

• **Monument to Gral. San Martin.** You will find it in the area nearest to Santa Fe Ave. Conceived by French sculptor Joseph Daumas as a simple marble pedestal on which the statue stood, it was later set upon a great red granite platform ornamented with allegorical figures and bronze reliefs. Responsible for these modifications was German artist Gustav Eberlein, who also changed the position of the statue. Formerly, San Martin pointed east; now, a 90° twist has made him face north, towards the stage of his liberating campaigns.

Monument to Gral. José de San Martín
The country first statue is today the scene
of all patriotic rallies.

"La Duda" (The Doubt)
An interesting sculpture in Plaza San Martin

• **Other Monuments.** Facing Marcelo T. de Alvear St., half hidden under the branches of a willow tree, you'll find *La Duda* (The Doubt). This marble sculpture belonging to the French classic period is by Louis Cordier and depicts an elderly man who seems to whisper something to a bewildered youngster. Across the street two small naturalistic bronzes can be seen: **El niño y la gallina** (The Boy and The Hen) by Nicolas Gulli, and **Grupo Infantil** (Child Group) by Vicente Gemito. On a corner near Florida St. stands a beautiful nude, known as **Fuente Catalana** (Catalonian Fountain) since it was a gift from that community. This statue was the center of an absurd story. Up until 1970 it stood in **Lezica Park**, where a group of shamefaced citizens, considering the naked figure outrageous because of its proximity to an image of the virgin, requested its removal. Fortunately the statue recovered its right to existence and was relocated at its present site. On the small Plaza Juvenilia (Florida, M.T. de Alvear and Santa Fe) stands the figure of **Esteban Echeverria** in tribute to one of the country's most eminent scholars. Back on the corner of Maipu and Juncal, the small monument to **Leandro N. Alem**, by Argentine sculptor Pedro Zonza Briano, was erected to honor this great national politician.

Kavanagh Building; Florida 1065 — You must have noticed it. It is that sort of stepped tower visible from any angle of the park, which appears and disappears through the trees making the most original and eyecatching piece of architecture in the area. When it was constructed, in 1934, it held the honor of being South America tallest building and the world's highest structure entirely made out of concrete. Built by architects Sanchez Lagos and De La Torre, the Kavanagh rises 30 stories and 120 meters high, housing 105 apartments with absolute privacy. Located on a corner at the highest point of the hill, this building has merged naturally into the physiognomy of Plaza San Martin as one of its most characteristic features.

Plaza Hotel; Florida 1005 — This elegant construction lined with bow windows, built in 1909 by German architect Alfred Zucker, is another eyecatching silhouette in the surroundings of Plaza San Martin.

Very often the Plaza is chosen by some conspicuous member of the international jet set and that is why, we suppose, it is somehow considered by the porteños the hotel par excellence, although the majority, for... obvious reasons, never went far beyond the lobby.

San Martin Park
Lost behind the trees, the outline of the elegant Kavanagh Building.

Iglesia del Santisimo Sacramento (Church of the Holy Sacrament); San Martin 1039 — Between the Plaza Hotel and the Kavanagh there is a short private alley that leads to San Martin street and the entrance to the church. This temple is not very large but certainly lavishly sumptuous. Note the main altar, a grandiose white marble structure with onyx, mosaic and bronze decorations, which occupies the whole width of the presbytery. The Holy Sacrament's is a favorite amongst the upper classes of Buenos Aires.

Circulo Militar (Military Circle); Santa Fe 750 — This building, originally the home of Jose C. Paz, founder of the newspaper "La Prensa" and dean of Argentine journalism, stands as a symbol for a crucial period in the history of our country.

It was then 1902. Those were the golden days in which B.A. grew at full speed, in the shadow of its agropecuarian wealth and in the light of European civilization. Both eloquently made evident by the magnificence of the palace, designed by French arch. Louis Sortais —who never visited B.A.— and built by his Argentine colleague Carlos Agote.

San Martin Palace, site of the Foreign Relations Ministry
A manorial building for a sumptuous retinue. And viceversa.

The residence is of course French from its foundations right up to the smallest piece of masonry, responding to that classical style dictatorially imposed by the famous Ecole des Beaux Arts de Paris. It occupies a surface of 12,000 square meters, 80 persons were at some time in charge of its maintainance, and although it was visited by the Prince of Wales and the Maharaja of Kapurtala among other prominent people, it was never inhabited by its owner.

• **Museo de Armas** (Arms Museum); Maipu corner of Santa Fe. The Paz Palace being nowadays the see of the Military Circle, it is not open to the public, but on the same premises a nice museum can be visited. Never mind if you are not interested in war and weapons. A collection of chinese dolls in exquisite typical attires is worth viewing, as well as the uniforms used by the Argentine army at different periods of its history. And there is also a Venetian armour that is quite something. (*Wednesdays to Fridays 3 to 7pm.*)

Palacio San Martin (San Martin Palace); Arenales 761

— Built by architect Alejandro Christophersen for the Anchorena family, this mansion was first named after its owner; it changed to San Martin Palace when it was sold to the State and became the Foreign Affairs Ministry.

Unlike the Paz Palace, this residence was actually lived in; three families occupied independent apartments looking onto a central patio, joined at the first floor by a covered circle. You may take a peek from the main gate.

The internal unification can hardly be noticed from the outside, but the differences in style cannot be disguised on the three fronts of the building. While the sector on Esmeralda goes almost unnoticed to the passerby, and the main entrance (Arenales St.) is an imposing baroque facade, on Basavilbaso St. you'll encounter a charming little corner all glass, ironwork and greenery, a parisian look which B.A. has taken as its own with no less authenticity than the tango and a good bife (steak). The best perspective is afforded coming up from Libertador Ave. towards Arenales.

Barrio Norte (Northern Quarter) — These buildings of noble architecture, mostly in French styles, are frequently seen all over the northern quarter. A good example are those surrounding the Plazoleta Carlos Pellegrini (Alvear Ave., Arroyo, Libertad), where you can see the French Embassy (Cerrito

1399), the Brazilian Embassy (Arroyo 1130) and the Jockey Club on Av. Alvear 1345. Another street with good testimonies of the city at the beginning of the century is Av. Alvear. At 1605 you will encounter the Apostolic Nunciature, a magnificent palace worthily accompanied by two others heroically withstanding the push of modern towers.

A stroll through this area will be enough to show you why this quarter is considered the center of elegance and luxury in Buenos Aires.

The Isaac Fernandez Blanco Museum
A corner of the baroque Spain in the center
of the northern residential quarter
of Buenos Aires.

Museo de Arte Hispanoamericano Isaac Fernandez Blanco (The Isaac Fernandez Museum of Spanish and American Art); Suipacha 1422 — You are not standing in front of an ancient restored house, as a first glimpse might indicate. This colonial like residence was built in 1925 by arch. Martin Noel at a time when an americanistic movement was in vogue in B.A., that brought about a revival of Spanish colonial styles by way of which the national feelings were supposed to be strenghened.

In 1936 the building was sold to the Municipality and became the Museo de Arte Colonial. Thanks to many donations, in 1947 the Isaac Fernandez Blanco Museum of Spanish and American Art was constituted, in honor of its most important patron. At present it is considered one of the most complete american art museums in the world.

Silverware. A stunning collection of silverware is treasured in this museum. The most elaborated religious implements and the commonest domestic utensils dating back to the XVIII century make up one of the finest sets of artwork ever to be seen.

The collection of artistic mates (little pots in which the yerba infusion is drunk) is particularly important. Each mate is accompanied by its corresponding bombilla (sucking tube) as well as by a portable water heater specially used to prepare the infusion.

The Peinetones (Large hair combs). A delicious example of old fashioned habits are the peinetones, huge shell combs which no lady in the past mid century would have dared to neglect. Due to their enormous size (some even got to measure one meter in width), writers and painters of the time made them the object of juicy satires. Anyhow, whether ridiculous or not, the peinetones became such a refined contrivance that they certainly deserved being included in an art museum.

Woodwork. The museum reaches one of its highlights in the field of decorative art, furniture and cabinetwork in general. Pieces of American and Argentine origin are on exhibition in colonial style reconstructed rooms which add realism to the show.

Paintings by Argentine artists, coin collections, ceramics and a more than complete library make a visit to the Fernandez Blanco a must.

Open everyday 3 to 8 pm.

*XVIII century silver mate
Fernandez Blanco Museum.*

Retiro was formerly the name for the whole northern area next to the river bank. Today, only the lowland at the foot of Plaza San Martin is known as such.

Where once the Gas Company and the Gunpowder Factory stood, we nowadays find the railroad station that houses the Mitre, Belgrano and San Martin lines. Lately, the bus terminal has been constructed, changing the looks of the whole sector.

The Sheraton Hotel and the new Catalinas Norte building complex, with its spectacular glass towers, have also contributed in more than a way to turn this side of the city into a new tourist attraction and an ever expanding commercial center.

WHERE TO EAT IN THIS AREA

AU BON AIR - Tres Sargentos 496
CANTINA CHINA - Maipú 967
CATALINAS - Reconquista 875
DOWN TOWN MATIAS - San Martin 979
EL ALJIBE (Hotel Sheraton) - San Martin 1225
HOSTERIA DEL CAB. BLANCO - M.T. de Alvear 479
JUNCAL ABAJO - Juncal 748
LAS NAZARENAS - Reconquista 1132
LES BROCHETTES - Arroyo 872
LIGURE - Juncal 855
ORIENTE EXPRESS (Harrod's) - Florida 877
SUBITO - Paraguay 640, 1°
TASKA TANCAT - Paraguay 645
VIEJA PANADERIA - 25 de Mayo 597, 1°

Torre de los Ingleses (The English Tower); Plaza Fuerza Aerea, in front of Retiro Station (Mitre Line) — This gift from the English residents in Argentina dates back to 1916. Designed by Ambrose Poynter, the tower is of course unmistakeable British, from its red brick front and mullioned windows up to the clock, a huge sphere 4,50 m in diameter and bronze bells weighing 6 tons. Also the materials, as well as the technicians and workers, were brought from England. The tower rises 76 meters high with 8 stories.

Catalinas Norte
In the site of the former Santa Catalina Convent
lies nowadays this new complex of modern skyscrapers.

The English Tower
A rithmycal counterpoint among the palm tree,
the Kavanagh building and the Tower.

Totem Canadiense (Canadian Totem Pole); Plaza Republica del Canada — This native Canadian totem pole is surely one of B.A. most original monuments. A replica of the totem worshipped by the Kwakiutl tribe of Vancouver, it is made of red cedar wood, rises 20 m high, and weighs 4 tons. The animals, 7 huge geometrical figures painted red, white and black, are represented in the order established by the myth, that is: an eagle at the top, then a sea lion, followed by a nutria, a whale, a beaver, a bird of prey, and at the very bottom, the head of a man.

It is sad to say that this monument stands a bit out of the way and few porteños know of its existence. You will find it only a few hundred yards behind the English Tower, towards the river.

The Canadian Totem Pole
Lower part of the Kwakiutl tribe's totemic pole
showing a man's head and an eagle.

Museo Ferroviario (Railroad Museum); Av. Libertador 405 — Inside the railroad grounds, in what used to be a warehouse of the Mitre line, a small but very interesting museum is open. A large glimpse of the Argentine railroads history can be obtained through items such as telephones, lanterns and even complete bathrooms belonging to the train stations of the past. *Mondays to Fridays 8 am. to 6 pm.*

FLORIDA STREET

All streets surrounding Plaza San Martin are a nonwritten invitation for a walk, but none like Florida.

It was called Calle del Empedrado (Cobblestoned Street), since it was one of the first streets in the city to be cobblestoned, but it also bore the names of San Jose, del Correo, Unquera and others. Till they got to Florida, on which everybody agreed.

Many important events —both great and small— took place here. A distinguished lady by the name of Mariquita Sanchez de Thompson y Mandeville, for instance, lived on Florida and it was at her house where the cords of the national anthem were first played. A plaque at 261, now an office building, reminds you of the historical episode.

Also Ana Diaz, the first woman arrived to our country, lived on Florida. Her house was at the corner with Corrientes Ave., where you can now see a building of curious ghotic lines; or rather the upper half of it, the lower part being a modern shop.

Although it was travelled by wagons and chariots, Florida has always been a pedestrian street. And a street for multitudes, too. From the very beginning it was the path to the bullfights in Plaza San Martin; later, the scene of military parades, funeral processions, royal retinues and dancing parties as well. Intellectuals, sportsmen, politicians, businessmen and everybody with a name in B.A. vaunted their fame strolling along Florida. It wasn't unusual to run into Mitre, Alvear or Mansilla on their way to work or just passing by.

Until World War II, Florida had a belle-époque touch which of course doesn't exist any more. Still in existence however are some bookstores (El Ateneo, # 340), as well as tearooms (Richmond, # 468) and traditional department stores (Harrods, # 877, James Smart, # 499). But the mansions have disappeared and the remaining ones vegetate anonimously or masked behind a commercial décor.

And yet, Florida has magic, still enchanting the tourist in its three different sectors.

• **From Plaza San Martin to Av. Cordoba**, Florida retains almost untouched its high-class essence of the old times. This is where you will find the most elegant —and expensive— boutiques, fashionable cafes, and that cosmopolitan, sophisticated and at a time bohemian spirit which seems so perfectly fit for 'the street of the country', as it was nicknamed.

At the corner of Cordoba, the **Centro Naval** (Navy Center) is well worth your time to look at. This lavish building by architects Dunant and Mallet treasures a wonderful ironwork in its front gate and all around the socle.

• **Between Cordoba and Lavalle**, Florida changes its face to a strictly commercial one. It is in this sector where the typical street arguments and discussions arise, turning the street into a popular forum. You will also encounter a lot of musicians, actors and jongleurs here —amateurs, needless to say— especially at night.

By now you have reached the **Galerias Pacifico** (Pacific Arcade), with entrance on 753. This cross-shaped building used to have openings also onto Viamonte, Cordoba and San Martin streets, but now those passageways have been closed. The only one open, onto Florida, gives access to the **Centro Cultural Las Malvinas** (Malvinas Cultural Center), where art exhibitions and cultural activities take place.

Like many other buildings in B.A., this one too was riddled with accidents. In 1889 it was designed to be a department store similar to the famous Galeries Lafayette in Paris. Economical difficulties changed its destiny, and painters, artists and art societies slowly started to settle in; even the National Fine Arts Museum had for some time its see there. Unproductive as it was, the Bon Marché (its original name) had to be put up for sale; it was purchased by the Pacific Railway (now San Martin line), hence the name with which it came to our time. In 1946 architects Aslan and Ezcurra completed the unfinished building, creating a commercial center that was a forerunner in its type and a model of good taste. Five great Argentine artists —Spilimbergo, Berni, Castagnino, Urruchua and Colmeiro— were appointed to decorate the 500 square meter dome, and with these mural paintings the Galerias Pacifico got its perfect finishing touch.

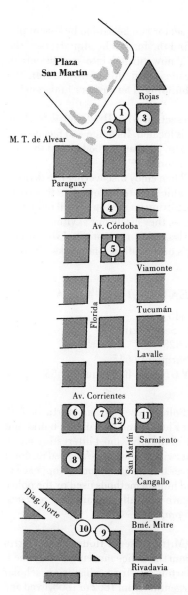

Plaza
San Martín

Rojas

M. T. de Alvear

Paraguay

Av. Córdoba

Viamonte

Florida

Tucumán

Lavalle

Av. Corrientes

San Martín

Sarmiento

Cangallo

Diag. Norte

Bmé. Mitre

Rivadavia

1. *Edificio Kavanagh*
2. *Plaza Hotel*
3. *Iglesia Smo. Sacramento*
4. *Centro Naval*
5. *Galerías Pacífico*
6. *Casa Gótica (Ana Díaz)*
7. *La Nación (ex sede)*
8. *Casa Mariquita Thompson*
9. *Banco de Boston*
10. *Monumento a R. S. Peña*
11. *Museo Policial*
12. *Casa/Museo Mitre*

• The last few blocks, **between Lavalle and Rivadavia**, have its own taste of austerity, may be because of the proximity to the financial district. However, Florida doesn't really loses its charm.

The architecture in this sector can be said to be sort of picturesque. At 343 you will find the former headquarters of the newspaper **"La Nacion"**, now turned into a commercial gallery. Its eyecatching facade is evidently borrowed from the Peruvian colonial style of building. The author of this work is arch. Pirovano.

Further on, at the intersection with Diagonal R.S. Peña (Norte), the **Boston Bank** is located. Its dome and facade won the municipal award in 1925, so just have a good look at the precise sculptural work decoration.

More architectural fun? Then enjoy discovering **the domes** of Buenos Aires, plenty of which are to be found on this corner and surrounding streets. Sitting on the top of civil buildings —not churches or temples—, they circle our skyline with the most diverse shapes and styles, creating an original view which certainly is one of the city's outstanding landmarks.

WHERE TO EAT IN THIS AREA

ABC - Lavalle 545
ALEXANDRA - San Martin 774
BLAB - Florida 325
CLARK'S II - Sarmiento 645
THE LONDON GRILL - Reconquista 455

Museo Policial (The Police Museum); San Martin 353, 7° and 8°f. — Just a block off Florida and lost among banks and travel agencies, stands one of the city's most interesting museums. If you are over 15 (otherwise you won't be allowed in) don't miss it. The endless resources used by delinquency, opposed to the ingenious technical and human methods used by the police in the prevention of crime are carefully explained here. *Tuesdays to Fridays 2 pm. to 6 pm.*

Casa-Museo Mitre (Mitre Museum House); San Martin 336 — Across the street from the police museum is an ancient colonial house in which Bartolome Mitre, a historian, scholar and journalist who ruled Argentina from 1862 to 1868, lived and died.

The architectural line, along with furniture, paintings, books and personal belongings are kept intact. A beautiful gate, good example of ironwork of the XVIII century, will lead you to the first patio, where a lifesize bronze statue of Mitre by Argentine sculptor Lucio Correa Morales seems to welcome the visitor.

On entering the second patio, an old curb of a well stands out among palm trees and other plants. The upper floor offers Mitre's private apartment, one of the most outstanding corners to visit in this house. On the same floor you will find the library, specialized on American subjects, and one of the most complete in the country. *Wednesdays to Sundays 3 pm to 7 pm.*

HOW TO GET THERE

Subway: Line C - SAN MARTIN station.

Buses: Lines 5, 7, 9, 10, 17, 26, 28, 33, 45, 50, 70, 92, 93, 101, 106, 108, 115, 130, 132, 150, 152.

Pacific Gallery
Sector of the dome towards San Martin St., painted by Spilimbergo.
Similar decorations can be seen facing Florida, the work of Castagnino.
(The Confiteria doesn't exist any longer).

It all started here, in Plaza de Mayo, the site chosen by Juan de Garay when he founded Buenos Aires.

A space was reserved around it for the Cathedral, another for the Cabildo (City Hall) and a third for the Fort. The city was small, scarcely 144 blocks with only 30 built upon. There was water on three sides and open country on the fourth.

This small nucleus grew to proportions that nobody could have suspected, until it became the great metropolis it is today. But Plaza de Mayo and the Southern District, with 400 years of history to their credit, will always be the heart of the city; getting acquainted with them is therefore not only necessary, but no doubt interesting as well.

PLAZA DE MAYO

Plaza de Mayo (May Square) occupies at present an extension of 20,000 square meters, but Garay allotted it with only half that size, that is, just the block made up by the streets which today we call Rivadavia, Bolivar, H. Yrigoyen and Defensa.

The other half went to the Jesuits and then to a small military garrison. The Plaza de Armas (Parade Ground), as it was named, and the Main Square were thus joined and both formed a huge open space which served for the most disparate needs.

To make the story short, that was just a great big dump. Market place, parking lot for carts, washerwomen's meeting corner, road to the jail, occasionally bullfight arena, dead animals on the way, excrement everywhere... And to top it all, the gallows in the place of honor, for the fun of bored neighbors and as a good example to schoolchildren.

Such a deplorable situation seemed to find a remedy when, in 1803, a sort of arcade was built to host the merchants' stalls, up until then located out in the open. This gallery cut right the square in the same direction of what today are Reconquista and Defensa streets, and so the site was again divided in two. The western side was called Plaza de la Victoria (Victory Square), the other half became Plaza 25 de Mayo.

In 1811, the erection of the May Pyramid led the way to further grooming of the place. In 1870 two gorgeous bronze fountains were settled; three years later the statue of General Belgrano is uncovered.

In the meantime, the surrounding buildings had improved, many were two stories high and began to be called 'altos' (the high ones). The Cathedral was finished, the Colon Theatre (the former one) had been built, and the Cabildo, although a bit run down, was all the same an important construction which gave prestige to the spot.

The plaza remained unchanged until 1884, but then a great remodellation was undertaken by Mayor Torcuato de Alvear.

1. *Cabildo*
2. *Catedral*
3. *Casa Rosada*
4. *Manzana de las Luces*
5. *San Ignacio*
6. *Santo Domingo*
7. *San Francisco*
8. *Museo de la Ciudad*
9. *Museo Etnográfico*
10. *Casa de Liniers*

The old gallery was pulled down, Defensa was closed off, the Pyramid went to the center of the grounds, the fountains were removed (now they can be seen at the crossing of Cordoba and Av. 9 de Julio), trees and flower beds were added.

And there we have Plaza de Mayo —its definite name after so many comings and goings—, once again with its original big expanse, a silent witness of four centuries of history.

The plaza today

Numerous and radical were the transformations which Plaza de Mayo went through since the days of the Spanish rule.

The oval outline which replaced its old rectangular shape, the opening of Av. de Mayo and the North and South Diagonals with their new perspectives, are urbanistic features which place the square into a clear baroque design, far from the Renaissance look of its early beginnings.

Pedestrians will no longer stumble over rotting rubbish but rather encounter hundreds of doves on their path. People seat-

May Square
A view of H. Yrigoyen St., lined with tall buildings.
It was here where street merchants offered their
goods in stalls called bandolas.
Their unscrupulous activities gave way to the word
bandolero to designate a brigand or thievish individual.

ed on the benches are not awaiting for some macabre execution, they are simply enjoying the sun or having a break in their jobs. The 'altos' have become important office buildings, embassies and State houses...

But not everything is lost. The essence of Plaza de Mayo lives on, rooted and silent, in its monuments and buildings, and to these we shall now refer.

• **Piramide de Mayo** (May Pyramid). Its official name was Columna del 25 de Mayo, its shape is that of an obelisk. But as it turned out, neither column nor obelisk were names which were going to catch on, and so it was outrightly decided that "the thing" being built in Victory Square was a pyramid and that was that.

The "thing" was the first patriotic monument of the country, erected to commemorate the events of 1810. Notwithstanding that, and since funds were scarce, it was thought that a simple wood and plaster contrivance in the shape of an obelisk (anything egyptian was in fashion in Napoleon's time) would do.

The May Pyramid
First patriotic monument of Argentina.

Fortunately, an intelligent man lived in B.A. —Juan Antonio Gaspar Hernandez was his name— and he was of the opinion that bargains are expensive in the long run, and that very little more money would afford a less ephemeral monument.

His advice was heard and the job given to Francisco Cañete, who built a modest structure of plastered brick over a three-step base, with a ball crowning the top, the whole surrounded by an iron railing to prevent carts from running into it or dogs mistake it for a tree, vegetation still laking in the bare expanse of the plaza.

In 1856, however, the pyramid was screaming for urgent repair. The task went to Prilidiano Pueyrredon, who retouched the moulding, enriched the sides with embossements and had four allegorical statues placed at each corner of the pedestal.

A fifth statue, representing Liberty, replaced the old spherical crowning. This figure, made by French sculptor Joseph Dubourdieu, seems shorter than its real height when seen from the foot of the monument; it is enhanced, on the contrary, if looked at from afar. A good point of view is the corner of Balcarce and H. Yrigoyen.

Buenos Aires kept on growing and by 1878 the pyramid seemed unworthy to represent it. Many thought it should be demolished altogether. Instead, it was remodelled by replacing the four statues with luxurious marble figures that had formerly ornamented other buildings.

After the demolition of the old gallery in 1884, the destiny of the Pyramid was once again uncertain. Finally, the marble figures were taken away and the monument placed in the center of the square. And there it has remained until now.

• **Manuel Belgrano Statue**. It stands just in front of the Government House. It might seem strange this place was chosen, since it does not have its balancing figure at the other end of the square, but this is so because the sculpture was unveiled in 1873, when the Plaza was still divided in two; obviously, the statue occupied Plaza 25 de Mayo.

The monument shows Belgrano turning on his saddle to contemplate the flag he created and holds in his right hand. The author of this work is French sculptor Albert Carrier-Belleuse and the modelling of the horse is by Argentine artist Manuel de Santacoloma. Owing to the considerable height of the monument, his work cannot be thoroughly appreciated, which is really a pity.

Metropolitan Cathedral; Rivadavia and San Martin —
It would take endless pages to detail all the hardships suffered
by the Cathedral of Buenos Aires till it reached its final state.
Of the eight constructions planned and executed, the early ones
were lost due to precarious materials or unskilful workers. The
fifth, in 1622, was a bit more solid, but still it wasn't enough.
Collapses, repairs and demolitions went on as usual.

In 1752, the bishop decides to take the matter seriously and
commissions Antonio Masella, an architect from Turin, the construction of the new temple. Once the building is finished, in
1791, B.A. can finally boast a Cathedral worthy of that name.

Only the **portico** was lacking, and to have it, another 30
years were to elapse. But the times had changed. While the
Cathedral was built during the colonial period, when the city
moved in the orbit of Spanish culture, with its religious roots
and not very fond of classical art, the portico dates back to
1822/27, after the May Revolution and with everybody looking
at France, which meant to chose progress. Logically then, two
Frenchmen were appointed for the task, Prosper Catelin and
Pierre Benoit, who achieved a beautiful row of 12 corinthian
columns upon which rests an entablature with a sculptured
pediment. Made by Joseph Dubourdieu in 1862, it represents
"Jacob meets his son Joseph in lands of Egypt", a subject al-
lusive to national reconciliation between provincials and porteños after a long period of disputes and armed confrontations.

A wonderful sight of the Cathedral is obtained from the corner of H. Yrigoyen and Bolivar, where the incongruence of the
portico with the dome appearing behind is self-evident.

Interior. Spacious and clear, your first impression on entering the Cathedral will be one of light and airiness. The temple
is composed of a nave and two aisles in which ample chapels
open out; as they are interconnected with each other, they make
the space seem even larger. The Cathedral actually covers an
important surface, aproximately 96 by 46 meters, since it was
Masella's idea to outbuild all other churches in Buenos Aires.

The **main altar**, a huge gilded carving of majestic proportions, will immediately outstand once you enter the Cathedral.
It was made in 1780 by Isidro Lorea, one of the best carvers of
the colonial period, in a lovely rococo style.

On the left arm of the transept you will find an altar with an
image traditionally known as the **Santo Cristo de Buenos
Aires** (St. Christ of B.A.). It is a life-size statue of polychromed
carob wood representing Christ on the cross before his death,

*Buenos Aires Metropolitan Cathedral
Neoclassical facade by Benoit and Catelin. Sculptured pediment
by Joseph Dubourdieu.*

with his eyes open. The artist has partially covered the figure with a loin cloth, following Spanish tradition. Another detail showing its ancient conception is that the Christ is of the so called "four nails" type, a formula which had long disappeared and been substituted by the figure with three nails, more stylized.

The author of this image, the oldest made in the River Plate (c.1670) and, according to experts, the most beautiful Christ we have in Argentina, is Portuguese carver Manuel Couto, who achieved an exquisite artwork at a time when B.A. was only an infinitesimal point on the maps of the world.

Further on, and still on the left hand aisle, you will see an altar dedicated to the **Virgen de los Dolores** (Virgin of Grief). The image arrived from Cadiz in 1752, clad in a splendid red velvet gown, but now it has a black one, made by ladies and girls devoted to *vestir santos* (dressing saints), a task that in ancient times was in charge of women who could not fulfill their religious vocation for lack of sufficient convents; hence the saying *Se quedó para vestir santos* (She was left to dress saints) which in Argentina was the typical phrase to designate old maids. Except this detail, everything in the Dolorosa is original.

• **Mausoleum of General San Martin**. You will find it at the fourth chapel of the right hand aisle. It was constructed in 1880 by Carrier Belleuse, who expensively used marble, going against the colonial esthetics that preferred wood or colored whitewashed fronts. Red and rose are the colors of the front, black the casket and white the three feminine figures that embrace the octogonal pedestal, representing Argentina in the center, Chile and Peru on the right and left, in clear symbolism to American unity accomplished by San Martin.

Because of the great size of the mausoleum, the chapel had to be enlarged with the addition of an antichamber. Still it came out rather narrow and the observer is compelled to view the monument at close range, which unfortunately is not the ideal distance to appreciate it correctly.

There is little more to be seen in our Cathedral. Relocations, losses and fires did away with several pieces, and those left are the work of underrated artists with no artistic value.

However, if nothing really good is to be found upwards, look down and there you'll see an exquisite piece of art: the mosaic of the floor, whose minute cubes represent thorns, nails and other motives of the Passion, forming a beautiful multicolored carpet throughout the church.

Cabildo (City Hall); Bolivar 65 — Of the three buildings projected by Garay, only the Cabildo still keeps an unmistakeable colonial look inspired on the ancient european city halls of the Middle Ages.

Built by Jesuit architect Andres Blanqui, it consisted of two double-storied wings at each side of a central towered construction. A series of arches on both floors, five on each side of the central block, formed the typical *recova* (archway) of colonial architecture, doubled by a gallery on the upper level. A great wooden balcony stressed the horizontal layout of the building. Red tiled roofing and whitewashed walls completed its characteristic Spanish look.

In other words, the same structure you can see today, except for a small great difference: why are there only five arches? What happened to the original eleven?

They were simply chopped off when Av. de Mayo and Diag. Sur were opened; furthermore, a supposed improvement had turned the austere old building into a neo-Renaissance pastiche overburdened with ornaments, which demanded the tower be sacrificed.

The Cabildo (Buenos Aires ancient City Hall)
In the background, the building of the Municipality.
It dates back to the beginning of the century
and the comparison is eloquent.

Thus mutilated, disguised and underestimated, the Cabildo survived until 1933, when a restoration undertaken by architect Mario Buschiazzo gave it back the aspect which very likely had in 1821. After that year, the Cabildo has no longer functionned as a government institution.

Interior. Here you will be rewarded with furniture, paintings and objects which are true treasures of the viceroyal period up to the May revolution.

In the Entrance Hall, watercolors by Carlos Enrique Pellegrini will give you an idea of what the old B.A. looked like; objects and furnishings provide also a lively image of the colonial way of life in the XVIII c.

The religious mind of the porteños in the colonial age is well reflected in the Religious Art Hall, where a beautiful baroque altarpiece dating back to the Jesuit Missions can be appreciated.

The Invasions Hall (left of the entrance) has mementos of the British incursion of 1806, as well as a large oil by Charles Fouqueroy showing the criollos' victory. A collection of ancient coins is another landmark in the ground floor.

On the staircase leading to the first floor you will see portraits of the Viceroys that governed the River Plate before 1810; you will pass the Sala de Mayo y de la Independencia (May and Independence Hall), with original prints made in B.A.'s first printing press, and finally you will arrive to the **Sala Capitular** (Chapter Hall), where the oath to the first argentine government was taken. Owing to its historical importance, this hall was accurately restored, although only the benches are original.

The Cabildo Museum
Reception Hall with colonial furnishings.

If you want to see more original items, just go out on to the right gallery, where a good collection of doors and ancient knobs are exhibited, among which the original Cabildo door.

Once outside, in the center of the patio you will be surprised by the well that belonged to Belgrano's home. And, last but not least, soldiers of the patrician regiment in their colorful attire serving as guardians of the Cabildo. *Mondays through Fridays 10 am. to 1 pm.; Tuesdays through Fridays and Sundays from 3 to 7 pm.*

Government House; Balcarce 50 — On the eastern side of Plaza de Mayo, the government house occupies the whole width of the square.

It started out as a fort, though it soon proved useless as the shallowness of the river made it difficult for the deep water vessels to get even near the shore. Consequently the fort only complied with symbolic functions and served mainly as lodging quarters for the authorities.

In 1855, part of the building became the city's customs office, the government retaining only a small portion on the corner of Balcarce and Rivadavia. The rest, slowly but systematically, started to deteriorate, crumble, catch fire and disappear.

In 1873, while Sarmiento was president, what was left of the building is demolished and the post office erected in the place. The small sector occupied by the authorities was repaired, somehow decorated with a few greenery, and a final face lifting was done with a good finishing touch of pink paint. From that day on, the government house became the *Casa Rosada* (Pink House).

Anyhow, the building was really in a bad condition, and in 1882 Pres. Roca decides to tear it down and build a new one. The new residence was built symmetrically to the post office, except for a loggia or gallery on the main floor that served as a balcony during parades.

In no time the building became too small for the increasing number of its occupants —burocracy, perhaps?— so that the post office is taken over.

Since a roofless alley remained between both constructions which was pretty annoying for the officials when going from one sector to the other, it was enclosed in a sort of great triumphal arch (Francisco Tamburini) that turned the two buildings into only one.

In the meantime, two more wings had been added and with

Government House.
For the porteños, the Pink House.

these the construction of the Pink House came finally to an end.

The result of so many changes and additions was a large building, mainly Italian in style but somewhat asymmetrical and with details of French origin, for instance the mansards. You will also note that the right side is quite a bit narrower than the other, as though a piece of it had been hacked. Well, actually something of the sort did happen. It was in 1938, when somebody thought of extending Av. de Mayo down to Paseo Colon. Hurriedly the works were started, but soon had to be stopped, as heated protests widely aroused. The torn down facade was rebuilt and the Government House finally managed to survive.

Museo de la Casa de Gobierno (Government House Museum); H. Yrigoyen 219 — Here you will see furniture, works of art, uniforms, awards and other items that belonged or are related to the governments of B.A. since its foundation.

But more interesting is perhaps the museum's setting, those underground galleries 15 meters deep, gloomy and mysterious.

They are the remains of the old fort; discovered by chance, it was decided to use the site for this original museum, presently under repairs. But it will open soon.

Old Customs House - Plaza Colon — Besides the museum, on the opposite side of the Government House, the former Customs House is also being unburied. Meanwhile, you can imagine its shape by observing the semicircular outline of Plaza Colon and Av. La Rabida, which follow exactly the curved border of the former building. In the center of Plaza Colon, the monument to Christopher Columbus, a gift from the Italian people to our city, can be seen.

Grenadier of the presidential guard.
The dazzling uniforms of this military corps
give a colorful touch to Plaza de Mayo
and the Government House.

*Monument to Christopher Colombus.
Entirely made out of marble by
Italian sculptor A. Zocchi.*

SOUTHERN QUARTER

Buenos Aires grew extending towards the south. Along Defensa and its adjacent streets, the aristocratic society took up residence, the religious orders built their churches, trade and culture prospered.

All this vitality would come to a drastic end when the yellow fever plague ravaged the city in 1871. The population in mass, especially the well-to-do families, started a true exodus in search of a healthier environment in the north, while the huge mansions left behind turned into disorganized tenement houses known as *conventillos*, soon taken over by the immigrants that were arriving by the thousands. And as the north undertook its career towards welfare and prosperity, the old *barrio* sank deeper and deeper into economic and cultural deterioration.

However, and perhaps from a slightly egoistic point of view, the whole process had its positive side to it, since a few historical buildings and sites have been preserved that otherwise might have been lost for ever.

The district today

The southern quarter is no longer what it used to be. The tourist seeking in B.A. an untouched historical center as other important capitals of the world are able to offer, may feel a bit disappointed.

Anyhow, a walk through the old streets where the first settlers of B.A. lived and built a new country, is a must in any well planned sightseeing program if the aim is to understand the city in its manifold aspects.

San Ignacio Church; Bolivar 225 — This church, the joint work of architects Kraus and Blanqui, dates back to 1723. Being the oldest temple in the city, it should display a pure colonial style, but it doesn't. On the contrary, and no doubt because of the bavarian origin of Kraus, it has a German look noticeable primarily in its narrow facade with high lateral towers and thick brackets on either side of the central archway. Only the right hand tower belongs to the original construction; as for the clock, it was intended for the Cabildo but was placed in San Ignacio's when the City Hall risked to be torn down.

Interior. It follows the Jesuit plan except for the presbytery, square-shaped instead of semicircular. The gilded wood main altar, baroque in style, was made by Isidro Lorea. Nuestra Señora de las Nieves (Our Lady of the Snows) one of B.A.'s most antique works (it is believed to date back to the XVI century) shouldn't be missed either. This typically Spanish figure can be found on the principal altar of the left hand aisle.

San Ignacio's was of great importance in the early B.A. and even provisionally substituted the Cathedral while the definite one was under construction. But one of the most curious events that ever took place in this church was undoubtedly to have been host to the first painting exhibition in B.A. In fact, owing to its importance, in 1823 San Ignacio's became the first art gallery in the city.

Manzana de las Luces (Square of Enlightment) — San
Ignacio is located within the boundaries of an illustrious block (Alsina, Moreno, Bolivar and Peru streets). Someone rightly called it Square of Enlightment on account of the many buildings related to the history and culture of the country that were established there.

The land was originally owned by the Jesuits, who apart from their temple erected there the Mission's Proctorship and the Company's school that would later become Colegio Nacional de Buenos Aires, one of the most prestigious in the city.

After the Jesuit order was expelled, the square went on being the city's center of intelectual development. The first printing shop, the House of Representatives, the Public Library and the University among other institutions, had their headquarters on this historical square.

The Tunnels — Not too long ago, an intricate series of underground galleries were discovered under the Square of Enlightment, which amazed both experts and profanes. Since these tunnels connected the Cabildo and the main churches of the early B.A., they are thought to have been constructed by the Jesuits as a means of defense... although an odd smuggler would have no doubt taken advantage of them now and then.

After years of restoration, the first sector can be visited in specially programmed tours. The starting point is at Peru 272. (*Please check exact date and time*)

San Francisco Church; Alsina and Defensa — This is

just another colonial church, although with so many alterations that it is difficult to recognize its original lines. Most of the altars belong to the first years of this century but an authentic antique can be seen at the altar of the right hand transept, made by an anonymous Portuguese carver of the XVII century. Take also a look at the pulpit, designed by Isidro Lorea, by now an old acquaintance of ours. Not a single straight line opposes to the graceful curves of this pulpit, by far one of the purest rococo exponents to be seen in Buenos Aires.

But the outstanding item in the nave is the big tapestry behind the main altar, a large cloth measuring 8 x 12 meters (second largest in the world), designed by argentine artist Horacio Butler to replace the original altarpiece, lost in a fire.

Finally, something that cannot be seen but is one of the greatest values of this church is its remarkable acoustics, which turns it into a perfect concert hall. If you have the chance to attend a performance while you are in B.A., you won't regret it.

Buenos Aires National College (Bolivar 263)
Many illustrious Argentine citizens graduated here.

Plazoleta San Francisco (St. Francis Little Square) —
Just in front of San Francisco's there is a small plaza where four
marble statues can be seen, standing at eye level. They are the
four sculptures of the May Pyramid taken away when the monument was relocated at the center of the square. They represent
Geography, Astronomy, Navigation, and Industry, and their neoclassic cut need not further comment, except that it was a
bright idea to withdraw them from our beloved and sober
pyramid.

A Colonial House; Defensa 183 — Known in its time as
Altos de Altolaguirre, that is, Altolaguirre Heights, this building is one of the city's true and authentic relics.

Two story houses were considered high class in colonial times
and the upper floor was usually topped by a *mirador* (observatory) that served as a lookout tower for pirate ships. Notice the
smooth walls, with the cornice that separates both levels as their
only ornament. But there is one detail —the walls ending at
straight angles on the corner— that will certainly arise your attention, since it has practically disappeared from B.A., as you'll
realize on your sightseeing through the city.

This historical house dating from the XIX century is currently under restoration and belongs to the City Museum, that is
only a few steps away.

WHERE TO EAT IN THIS AREA

CHEZ LOUIS (Hotel Nogaro) - Alsina 541
EL JABALI - Belgrano 538
FRANKFURT - Piedras 375
LA ESTRELLA DE ORO - Moreno 360
PEDEMONTE - Avda. de Mayo 676

Museo de la Ciudad (The City Museum); Alsina 412 —
All that regards the city's early life is waiting for you at the City
Museum. You'll be enchanted in seeing the old tiles that
adorned the porches of neighborhood houses as well as the
art of 'fileting', a porteño decorative genre of colorful
arabesque designs, very popular amongst cart owners when
they still trundled the city. Nowadays, horse drawn vehicles
have of course disappeared, but the filet style is still adopted

on some trucks and colectivos. Old postcards, pictures and ads from the beginning of the century will certainly give you a good laugh. *Sundays through Fridays from 11 am. to 7 pm., Saturdays 4 to 8 pm.*

Farmacia "La Estrella" (Estrella Pharmacy); Alsina 402 — On the ground floor of the City Museum you will find this still working drugstore, kept the way it was at the turn of the century. Once again a vision of the past is brought to our days in its carved walnut shelves and huge collections of flasks and jars under an allegorically depicted ceiling. La Estrella is an excellent example of investigation and conservation, worthwhile seeing.

Liniers House, at 69 Venezuela St.
Only its facade and a small part
of the interior are left.

Church of Santo Domingo; Defensa and Belgrano Av. — Of all churches that have reached our days, Santo Domingo's is the one that relates the most to B.A.'s history. During the British invasions of 1807, the English troops seeked refuge in this church and still today bullet holes can be seen on the left tower. The flags taken by Liniers (commander of the local forces) are kept in the Virgin's Chamber along with other mementos from the Independence battles.

The rest of the church is less warlike. Its beautiful interior, made up of three naves of excellent proportions, is by Antonio Masella —the author of the Cathedral. As in most churches of this period, it is sad to say that very little is left of its simple colonial architecture. Only the image of Magdalena Penitente (3rd. altar of the right-hand aisle) is inspired in Spanish models

Santo Domingo's Church
Reminders of the 1807 British invasions
can still be seen on the left tower.

of the XVII century. Even the table of the altar is a substitute, since the original was lost in arson. Out in the porch, you'll find Belgrano's mausoleum, a splendid monument built by the Italian artist Ettore Ximenes in 1897. Manuel Belgrano, the author of our flag, was born and died on the avenue that recalls his name and it was only logical that his remains should lie here.

A good piece of information? The organ at Santo Domingo's is the most important in B.A. and is often used in public concerts. Another musical landmark not to be sidestepped.

Ethnographic Museum Juan B. Ambrosetti;

Moreno 340 — What you are seeing is an authentic building of 1880 in the richest Italian style. Built by arch. Pedro Benoit jr., this construction was destined to the university, but in a short time it became too small and was granted to the School of Law until 1935, when it became a museum.

More than 150,000 pieces, some as old as a thousand years, are arranged in superb collections of enormous archaelogical, ethnographic and anthropological value. The material originates mainly from ancient American, Asian and African cultures; outstanding is the Argentine area, where you shouldn't miss the **Urna Quiroga** (Quiroga Urn), a unique piece that belonged to the Calchaqui tribe. *Tuesdays through Fridays 3 to 6 pm.*

HOW TO GET THERE

Subway: Line A - PLAZA DE MAYO station.
Line D - CATEDRAL station.
Line E - BOLIVAR station.

Buses: Lines 2, 24, 28, 29, 56, 64, 91, 93, 99, 105, 111.

Pulpit of San Francisco's Church
It is the most rococo work ever conceived during the viceroyal period.

Tour 3

Avenida de Mayo (May Avenue) is one of the city's most im-
portant thoroughfares. But its real meaning goes beyond that
simple fact. It symbolizes that moment in the history of Bue-
nos Aires when a small town, sunk in its colonial mentality, de-
cides to launch out and follow the paths and life projects of the
most advanced countries in the world. An ideal foreseen by the
men of May, ephemerally made true in Rivadavia's time, and
carried out to its ultimate consequences by the generation of
the eighties.

A little history

Avenida de Mayo has no before nor after. It was born ready-
made, and it was born right.

Its design is obviously borrowed from the great baroque european cities, in which significant buildings are linked by broad
avenues that tear across the urban network. This is what happened in the Rome of the XVII c., and in Paris when the famous
Baron Haussmann changed the face of his city in the last century's seventies.

Only 20 years later, Buenos Aires did likewise. The local
Haussmann was called Torcuato de Alvear and he was the most
progressive mayor the city ever had. The representative buildings to be connected were the government house and the congress, through a main artery to be known as Avenida de Mayo.
(Its center, at present, is exactly at the crossing with 9 de Julio
Ave; we suggest you stand there to obtain an excellent panoramic view towards both ends of the perspective.)

1. Cabildo
2. La Prensa
3. Café Tortoni
4. Tacuarí 17
5. Suipacha 50
6. Pasaje Rivarola
7. Hotel Chile
8. Crítica
9. Edificio Barolo
10. Pasaje La Piedad
11. Teatro Liceo
12. Plaza del Congreso
13. Congreso Nacional
14. Conf. del Molino

Avenida de Mayo
A view from the Pyramid towards the National Congress.

Such a daring project aroused of course a great deal of opposition among the population, specially when all blocks between Rivadavia and H. Yrigoyen had to be torn down, a job not always carried off with as much care as it might have been expected; such was the case, for instance, of the Cabildo, which lost a good portion of its right wing. But in the end progress pushed on and in 1894 the avenue was inaugurated.

This new urbanistic conception radically changed the look of B.A. and marked the starting point of a building craze almost never equalled in its history. Not only as for the number of houses constructed —13 blocks built up in only 16 years— but also because of the revolutionary turn in the architecture of the city that could be seen as from the birth of the Avenue.

In fact, up to 1880 B.A. had been a low town where only the domes of the churches outstood among the flat colonial structures. It is easy to imagine then the amazement of the porteños when five and six story buildings were erected before their eyes, with an overwhelming succession of slate roofs, lavish French ornaments, and countless balconies looking out onto sidewalks almost as wide as the old streets where horse drawn carts still were rumbling around.

Municipality of Buenos Aires.
Starting point of Avenida de Mayo.
(See ill. page 47).

How it came out

Just to get the feeling of these people, we invite you to the corner of Av. de Mayo and Bolivar St. To your left, the Cabildo, of pure colonial architecture; to your right, on numbers 525 and 575, the Town Hall building and the headquarters of La Prensa newspaper. It's unnecessary to stress the sharp contrast, it is simply a French transplant in the River Plate.

But these are only an example. All along the porteño boulevard you'll come across with representative buildings both in quantity and in quality. Just start walking, forget about the ground floors and their modernized shop windows (of doubtful taste), and concentrate on the upper half of the facades. You will be able to appreciate the uniformity in heights from one house to another, which add to the harmony of the whole, even if there are no two buildings alike. Some fronts have been restored and look magnificent; others have to put up with ninety years of grime, but hopefully by the time you read these pages a beautician might have reached them.

Some points of special interest — We have already mentioned La Prensa building. This construction, which houses one of the largest newspapers in the country, is crowned by a bronze feminine figure holding in her right hand a powerful lamp that can be seen from far away. In her left hand, a large piece of "paper" with the paper's slogan. La Prensa is also famous for its siren, which is only activated in case of serious news such as war, so it's better not to hear it often.

Following the pioneer example of La Prensa, journalism of all colors established their headquarters on Av. de Mayo. Unforgettable is Critica, a paper famous in the thirties for its modern journalistic conception and intelligent sensationalism. Critica was closed down, but the building by arch. Jorge Kalnay is still there, on number 1333.

• The Barolo Building. This block includes other important buildings, the most eyecatching being the Barolo, on 1370.

It is hardly impossible to classify the Barolo's architectural style. Is it baroque? Art Nouveau? Or Expressionist? It might be a mixture of a little bit of all and a lot of courage and imagination, which Mario Palanti, the author, had plenty of, according to the fanciful lines of his building.

With its 24 floors in height, the Barolo was at the time of its construction (1922) the tallest building in B.A. as well as the most popular landmark in the Av. de Mayo. And although it was shortly surpassed by the Mihanovich Tower in Arroyo St., it will always remain as the unmatched symbol of an age marked by ostentation and optimism.

Another building with a history to it stands at # 1317, on the corner with Sgo. del Estero St. This seven story construction housed the **Hotel Majestic**, one of the most luxurious in the Avenue. The famous dancer Nijinsky chose it for his wedding night, and French architect Le Corbusier was but another of the many guests of world fame that honored the place. The hotel is no longer on operation and has become headquarters of the Direccion General Impositiva (General Tax Bureau), also very famous amongst the porteños although, needless to say, for quite different reasons.

Just in front of the DGI stands the **Chile Hotel**, still working. It was and it is one of the best exponents of Art Nouveau on Av. de Mayo.

The people — Despite its refined architecture, Av. de Mayo never managed to grasp the honor of being called an aristochratic street, such as Florida or later Av. Alvear. On the contrary, it was always the favorite of the middle classes and specially the Spanish community, who little by little took over the avenue with their particular habits and idiosyncracies. *Chocolate con churros* (hot chocolate with crullers), *paella* (safron flavored dish of rice and seafood), *puchero* (a variety of boiled meat and assorted vegetables) and other specialities could be tasted at the many restaurants, bars and hotels spread all along the avenue and surrounding streets. Still today, it is in this area where the best of the Spanish cookery can be found. (See list of restaurants below).

WHERE TO EAT IN THIS AREA

EL GLOBO - H. Yrigoyen 1199
EL HISPANO - Salta 20
EL IMPARCIAL - Salta 97
LA CABAÑA - Entre Ríos 436
LAURAK BAT - Belgrano 1144
LOPRETE - Luis S. Peña 749
PERSEPOLIS - H. Yrigoyen 991

*Avenida de Mayo, corner of Santiago del Estero St.
One of the most splendid and representative
art nouveau buildings on the avenue,
currently being occupied by a hotel.*

The cafes — The arrival of the Spaniards brought about the
cafe with terrace; this would never have been possible in a city
of narrow streets, but it was quite feasible in such a broad
avenue that called for those endless chats which the Spaniards
are so fond of. Moreover, a small change would introduce the
personal touch to make it a local habit. Instead of putting the
tables leaning on the wall, like in the motherland, here it was
chosen to place them in the area closest to the curb, while the
free space up to the wall was used as a sort of corridor along
which pedestrians could walk.

Avenida de Mayo between 1300 and 1400
Along the last stretches of the avenue, French eclecticism
has given way to a diversity of styles
which can easily be noted in the picture.

   This out-door drawing room in which the Avenue had developed became in no time the meeting place par excellence, in
which numerous coffee shops appeared, some popular, some
luxurious, and some even literary, like the **Tortoni** —still open
today on 829— where prominent intelectuals such as Leopoldo Lugones, Alfonsina Storni or Alfredo Palacios would meet.

The avenue, today — After 1945, a great deal of that young thriving atmosphere disappeared. Fortunately, a restoration plan is being carried out, so that the Avenida de Mayo, which was "French by conception, Spanish by adoption and Porteña by conviction" will not contradict this slogan that has so acutely grasped the spirit of one of the richest in history streets in Buenos Aires.

PLAZA DEL CONGRESO

A few steps before reaching Luis Saenz Peña St., a large open space of three blocks known as Plaza del Congreso (Congress Square) marks the ending of Av. de Mayo.

Plaza Lorea — Of these three blocks that make up the Congress Square, the first is known as Plaza Lorea. Of course the name must sound familiar to you; in fact Lorea was the author of the main altarpiece of the Cathedral and was also the owner of this property.

You surely must be thinking that B.A. intended to pay homage to one of its most capable early sculptors by naming the plaza after him. But reality is not always as romantic as that. It so happens that Lorea, a rather egocentric man, donated the land under the condition that the square would perpetually carry his name. The Cabildo, obliged, just in case Mister Lorea changed his mind. However, his wish was complied partially since half of the area receives nowadays the name of Mariano Moreno. But no worry, there are no heirs to claim their rights.

On Plaza Lorea two large tiled stairways that seem to lead nowhere can be seen; in fact, they were the access to the public restrooms that were common to all parks in the past. The baths are gone and all that is left are the two classical signs reading *Señoras* and *Caballeros* (Ladies and Gentlemen).

• **Liceo Theatre**. Across the street, on the corner of Rivadavia and Parana, stands one of B.A.'s true relics: the Liceo Theatre. Known in the past as Goldoni, Rivadavia and Moreno among other names, the Liceo is one of our oldest theatre houses and except for a few alterations its original construction

is the same. It was here where Gregorio de Laferrère presented his famous comedy "*Las de Barranco*", a classic in argentine drama.

On the way to the Congress — After Plaza Lorea you
immediately reach Plaza Congreso. Unlike the former, which
in its origin was no more than a parking lot for wagons, Plaza
Congreso was exquisitely cared for from the very beginning,
since it was born to enhance the Congress building.

On the way to the Congress, a few stops are to be made. First,
before the impressive **"El Pensador"** (The Penseur), by Auguste Rodin. The statue had been part of two gigantic doors the
artist was making for a museum in Paris but were never concluded. The decoration's main theme was Dante's Inferno and
once the artwork was taken apart, the loose pieces went to private collections. Our Penseur is not the original, but almost,
since it is one of the only two largesize copies in the world. The
other is in New York.

Your second stop will be next to a modest monolith that
marks "Km 0" on the whole country's road system. The author
of this simple little work is none other than Jose Fioravanti,
responsible for such monumental pieces of sculpture as Roque
Saenz Peña's statue on Florida and Diagonal Ave., or the Avellaneda Monument in the neighborhood of Palermo.

• **Monumento a los dos Congresos** (Monument to the Two
Congresses). This is the largest monument in the whole area,
located in the third section of the square, after crossing Cevallos
Street. It was erected to honor the congress of 1813 (as a matter of fact an assembly, in which slavery was abolished) and the
one held in Tucuman in 1816 that declared national independence.

The authors of the work were Jules Lagae and Eugenio
D'Huicque, who conceived through the use of noble and lavish materials this important work of sculptural and architectural value.

To get an even better picture we suggest a walk around the
platform, that can be reached through any of its three perrons.
But probably the most decorative side is the one overlooking
Av. de Mayo, where an artistic fountain enhances the whole
square.

Congreso Nacional (The National Congress) — To the
west of the monument, National Congress stands. This build-

National Congress
Central part of the building dominated by its pear-like dome,
visible all along the Avenue.

ing, designed by architect Victor Meano, is of grecoroman style, as he himself defined it. In fact, it isn't but a mixture of greek and roman architecture with a decorative renacentist touch. Meano intended his building to be a monument worthy of a "young, free and vigorous nation" and in that he succeeded, mainly on account of its location as a drop scene to Av. de Mayo.

It is worthwhile noticing the dome, that at first sight might seem a bit narrow in comparison with the wide building's front. But, should it have been any wider, it would have obstructed the visual field, distorting its need as the ending point of the perspective. In this way, on the contrary, a perfect centralized view can be obtained.

As for the building's decoration, it seems to be inconcluse. Noticeable is the absence of carvings in the pediment or sculptures crowning the stairway of honor.

This sightseeing of the Congress you have made it from the Monument of the Two Congresses. Now, before descending we suggest you take a glimpse towards the river. From this vantage point you'll enjoy a wonderful and entirely new perspective of the Avenue at its full length and, far away, a fading minute silhouette between the double row of trees lined along Av. de Mayo, the Government House.

The surroundings — To finish off this tour, it is a good idea you stroll down the streets parallel to Av. de Mayo and observe the numerous old houses still standing there. The wear-and-tear is perhaps greater than that on the Av. de Mayo itself, but a clinical eye will help to discover some true hidden treasures.

One of these is **Pasaje de la Piedad** (Passage of Pity), a "U" shaped inner alley between numbers 1525 and 1573 of Bartolome Mitre St. Old manors of noble architecture, iron fences, porches with well kept gardens, pilings on the sidewalks where horses used to be tied... And silence, yes silence! right in the midst of the din of automobiles and horns, turn this spot into a touristic gem which can't be missed. We suggest you hurry and see it before someone decides it must be put up to date and pulled down.

Cortada Rivarola (Rivarola Passage) is a short dead end street only 100 meters long, stretching from Bme. Mitre to Cangallo on the 1300 block. Along Rivarola too, the houses have maintained their ancient appearance, with the curious peculiarity that the constructions are exactly the same on both sidewalks, facing each other as in a mirror.

Confiteria del Molino (Molino Coffee Shop) — And if
you feel like having a rest after all this walking around, take advantage of El Molino. Meeting place of legislators and stage of political rallies and debates, the Molino still keeps up a good deal of the city's tradition and history.

La Piedad passage (detail)
Peaceful, mysterious and suggestive,
it is a living document of the porteño architectonic past
and has been a setting of many national films.

"Del Molino" coffee house
A *"branch"* of the Congress where
most senators and deputies take a break.

HOW TO GET THERE

Subway: Line A - PERU, PIEDRAS, LIMA,
            SAENZ PEÑA and CONGRESO
            stations.
            Line C - AVENIDA DE MAYO station.

Buses: Lines 6, 7, 12, 23, 24, 37, 38, 39, 45, 50,
            56, 59, 60, 86, 102, 105, 150.

Tour 4

San Telmo
La Boca
Costanera Sur

Traditional places are not abundant in Buenos Aires. The need of progress and urban renewal has practically put an end to those old colonial constructions that so well fit into the way of life of the old city. The narrow streets, suitable for horses and carts, have been widened and paved to make way to automobiles; the low houses with sunny patios were humiliated at the feet of haughty palaces first, and by inhuman steel towers later.

Only the south resisted the change. But what is the south? This name is given, in Buenos Aires, to an extense zone including the districts of San Telmo, La Boca, Barracas, Parque Patricios, Nueva Pompeya, Monserrat, San Cristobal, and Constitucion among others.

An indefinite area with not very clear limits, the south has long left behind its fame as a tough neighborhood for which it became almost a legend. However, it is also true that, owing to various circumstances, these neighborhoods have often been left aside from the demographical shakings which caused the radical metamorphosis of other areas in the city. That is why, even if the benefits of progress have not entirely passed it by, the south always maintains that typical profile that makes it so appealing to tourists.

Of the vast number of suburbs mentioned, there are two where time seems to have stood still: San Telmo and La Boca, two names which often sound familiar to the tourists even before arrival. It is here, therefore, where we will find our starting point.

SAN TELMO

San Telmo in its beginnings was only a street. A path, a trail covering the distance between the main square and the port. Along this trail —the same known nowadays as Defensa St.— a heterogeneous population made up of carpenters, shipworkers, calkers and other portuary oriented labourers began to settle. Some black slaves and a pretty large number of undesirable elements completed the social scene of the zone.

Because it was on the coast's high ground, or perhaps because the caravans arriving at this point made a halt (an *alto*) in their journey, the truth is that the area, known since its early stages as San Pedro, rounded off its name and became, as from the XVII century, the Alto de San Pedro (The Heights (or Halt) of San Pedro).

That's how Buenos Aires acquired its first slum, a riverside suburb isolated from the privileges of the main square which, needless to say, grew with exasperating slowness.

Anyhow, the time came when the inhabitants were too many and a church was needed. There went the Jesuits and started the construction of Nuestra Señora de Belem (Our Lady of Bethlehem), later finished by the Bethlemite monks when the former were expelled from the River Plate.

But if the building of the temple was important, more so was the creation of an independent new parish in 1806. It was called San Telmo and from then on the Alto de San Pedro became simply San Telmo.

On entering the XIX century, the participation of the district in the community was pretty active. Its role during the British invasions was decisive. French and Beruti, the creators of our national emblem, were neighbours of San Telmo. So was Esteban de Luca, poet of the Revolution.

San Telmo was also —and that is probably its most praised reward— where the principal medical institutions established their headquarters. The first hospital in B.A., the Faculty of Medicine, great hospitals such as Rawson, Italian and British, were all, and some still are, in the southern zone.

And yet, paradoxically enough, the district of medicine and hospitals remained in other aspects in the most absolute backwardness. Not only inside those establishments did total ignorance prevail insofar as hygiene and asepsis. Unpaved roads, no running water nor sewer systems, mountains of garbage in empty plots, turned San Telmo into a gigantic infection focus that would lead to the worst epidemic diseases ever occurred in B.A., especially the yellow fever of 1870.

After that year, San Telmo was deserted. To the victims of the plague, the mass exodus of the survivors was added. But the tragedy proved also to be a warning, and as such was assimilated. For the first time in 300 years the district was cleaned up, the streets were paved, the worn out houses disappeared and the most urgent problems were solved or at least attended to.

In this process, much of the merit goes to the crowds of immigrants who filled the void left by the natives. It was their tenacity and hankering for progress which saved San Telmo from oblivion and helped creating its fame as a decent suburb of peaceful and laborious people.

San Telmo today

It is not easy to draw a dividing line between past and present San Telmo.

Up till the fifties, the district stuck to its characteristic image. Nothing had been touched; its winding roads, the untidy cobblestone, the old houses and patios, were all there, unchanged throughout the years.

All of a sudden, around the sixties, somebody discovers this hidden treasure and in no time the secret is proclaimed. Brought by romanticism, more often by commercial cunning, down swooped the pioneers and settled in the zone; ipso facto land prices began to rise, apartment buildings were hastely constructed, several streets were widened and paved...

However, to the logical rejoicing of the population, a certain rejectment among neighbours and authorities followed on seeing how that familiar surrounding, that jewel of the past, was rapidly running towards extinction. Consequently, more than one modernization program suffered a healthy delay.

Today, San Telmo has returned to its conservative rhytm, although a new attitude has split its face in a somewhat peculiar manner. During the day, the drowsy townlike atmosphere of the past is still there; at night and on weekends, a drastical change takes place and the 'din' starts; restaurants light up, cafes-concert, tango bars, artcraft shops, art galleries and off Corrientes shows make up a sophisticated little corner in the heart of B.A., a bit unusual perhaps but certainly a must for tourists in search of entertainment, culture and fun.

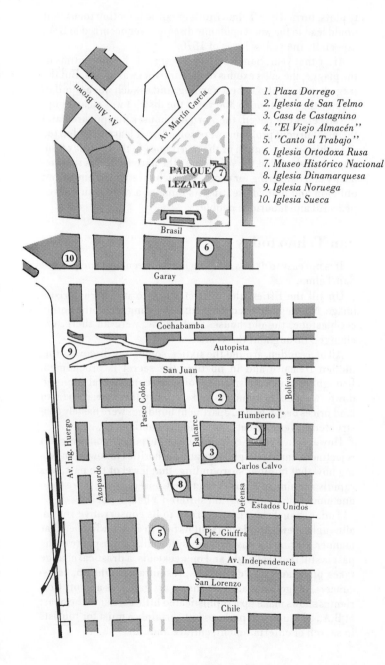

1. Plaza Dorrego
2. Iglesia de San Telmo
3. Casa de Castagnino
4. "El Viejo Almacén"
5. "Canto al Trabajo"
6. Iglesia Ortodoxa Rusa
7. Museo Histórico Nacional
8. Iglesia Dinamarquesa
9. Iglesia Noruega
10. Iglesia Sueca

Some old streets and houses — As you surely have realized after reading the above paragraphs, San Telmo must be walked through, and better still on weekdays during the day.

A good starting point is the corner of Independencia and Paseo Colon Avenues, where you'll find a beautiful perspective of the *Canto al Trabajo*, by Argentine artist Rogelio Yrurtia.

• **Canto al Trabajo** (Song to Labour). This is one of the most exceptional sculptures in B.A. Through 14 splendid bronze figures adopting different postures, the author has managed to convey a whole philosophy of life based on effort, love and confidence in the future. First of all, a huge rock being hauled by three men can be seen; then other groups follow, expressing with their hunched backs their submission face to an enslaving destiny. Finally, when the happy influence of woman and children appears in the life of a man, two upright figures clearly symbolize the deep meaning of work as the impelling force of progress and freedom.

"Canto al Trabajo" by Rogelio Yrurtia (detail).

Behind the sculpture, on Paseo Colon, you will see the classic columns of the Faculty of Engineering and, next to it, the building of the Ministry of Agriculture, quite opposed in style.

On Paseo Colon, though, you are treading the former lowlands of the coast, transformed into the tree-lined avenue it is today when Madero Port was constructed. The historical and true San Telmo which we are interested in, lies on the other side of the avenue, climbing the slope. And here you'll make several stops.

San Telmo
Old deterioated walls contrast with
the modern apartment building in the background.

On San Lorenzo 319 there is an interesting old house, open to the public since it is now a gallery where painters, ceramists and other artisans have established. Obviously the building has been done over, although without losing its original design, based on a characteristical feature in the porteño house of other times: the patio and, around it, the rooms.

The traditional porteño house. The patio was of the utmost importance in early Argentine architecture. According to their social level, all houses included one or more, each for a different purpose. The first was surrounded by the reception halls: living room, dining room and library; a short passage led to the second patio, larger than the first since it corresponded to the bedrooms. The third patio was for the servants quarters and usually included a small orchard, poultry yard and other out-buildings.

With time, immigration and economical crisis, this typical mediterranean design, brought to America with colonization, was reduced to half its size by cutting it lengthwise, thus leaving all the rooms aligned on one side and the patios on the other. That is how a large comfortable house became two smaller ones, which also meant, of course, that the owner had a chance to cash two rents... Porteños witfully called these homes *casa chorizo,* which literally means sausage house, a kind of construction that hasn't at all disappeared around the oldest suburbs of Buenos Aires.

Another very typical element of the ancient houses was the iron grates. Not a single window did not have them, making the homes totally independent from the outside. At the beginning they reached the ground and were very coarse; when the art of smelting improved, more complex and artistic designs appeared which reached excellent levels in front-door gratings, used to separate the entrance hall from the interior of the house.

In this one of San Lorenzo St. which we were commenting there is no such iron grating door, but if you should tour the old quarters of B.A. you will come across many examples of railings which are authentic fancy ironwork, as well as a great number of houses which respond to the described model. It is easy to recognize them: to one side is the door and, next to it, one or two windows indicate the main hall, after which the remaining rooms follow on.

Now, returning to San Lorenzo St., on the opposite sidewalk you'll see a curious remnant of a wall numbered 380. It is the narrowest house in B.A., measuring only 2.20 m wide. Legend has it that this type of minute living quarters were given to emancipated slaves by their former owners so that they could start a new life of their own.

Architectural relics are not lacking in San Telmo; one of these is the house on Balcarce 1016, where painter Juan Carlos Castagnino had his atelier. The house has been modernized in its interior but still retains its XVIII c. facade. Nowadays the building is an art gallery with a special hall dedicated to the painter and at night it becomes a theatre and a cafe-concert.

Round the corner, on Carlos Calvo St., you will find two houses with interesting stories. On number 319 it is said that Margarita Oliden lived. She was the lover of the chief of the *Mazorqueros* (dictator Rosas' dreaded secret police). At present the house has been turned into a good restaurant. Esteban de Luca, a poet of the Revolution, lived also on this street. His two hundred year old house is on number 383. A plaque informs you that the first arsenal in B.A. was here, although many historians have serious doubts about it.

An unavoidable corner is that of Balcarce and Independencia, on Balcarce 799. You have actually been there at the starting of this tour and no doubt noticed a low very white house with iron railings on the windows and the terrace. What you are viewing is "El Viejo Almacen", a tango-bar (restored) which was made famous by Edmundo Rivero, one of Buenos Aires' most cherished tango singers.

Many other streets in San Telmo have that particular San Telmo touch. The Pasaje Giuffra (between Independencia and Estados Unidos), Cochabamba, Defensa (a bit noisy but still enchanting), Humberto I, where the church that gave the neighborhood its name stands), Chile, Bolivar, and others. To walk them along and let your imagination make a jump into the past trying to discover their secrets, shall be entirely left up to you, to the flair and eagerness of the adventurous tourist you certainly are.

WHERE TO EAT IN THIS AREA

ADAM - Chile 274
ANTIGUA TASCA DE CUCHILLEROS - Carlos Calvo 319
AU COIN DE MARSEILLE - Defensa 714
EL REPECHO DE SAN TELMO - Carlos Calvo 242
LA CASA DE ESTEBAN DE LUCA - Defensa 1000
LA CREVETTE - San Juan 639
TABERNA BASKA - Chile 980
TARASCON - Carlos Calvo 547

An old house in San Telmo.
The well, the brick tiled patio and lots of
plants in pots and vines bring back a
romantic reminiscence of other times.

Typical colonial house (restored).
Windows down to the ground, iron railed terrace
and tiled roof projection.
Today it is a well known restaurant.

Plaza Dorrego (Dorrego Square) — While walking down Defensa, you'll reach a small plaza, or rather a simple cement square surrounded by a low brick wall. There is no vegetation here, except for two huge gum trees that embrace an ancient well. There will probably be a few children playing football and a couple of retired people talking away on the only two benches the place has to offer.

You have reached the exact spot where the carts going to and fro the port made a halt. In other words, the Alto de San Pedro.

It was also known as Plaza de la Residencia (Residence Square) because the Jesuits erected their buildings in the neighborhood, in 1822 it was renamed Plaza del Comercio (Commerce Square) owing to the activities that took place there, until finally in 1897 it became Plaza Dorrego.

By that time it was already historically important. Along with Plaza de Mayo, this one is the city's oldest plaza. It was here where independence was pledged only two months after it was proclaimed in Tucuman. In 1820, the Canto al Trabajo was placed in the square, but unfortunately the spot ended up being too small for such a huge monument, so that it had to be removed and the plaza was left alone once more.

• **Feria de San Telmo** (San Telmo's flee market). Quite solitary during the week, Plaza Dorrego becomes unusually crowded on Sundays and can be hectic when the flee market known as Feria de San Telmo takes place. Anything you can name, lots of handicrafts, vernacular silverware, are offered by merchants in the most incredible attires. In the surrounding streets, artistic or historical values are also very likely to be found.

Don't change your money in the streets. Argentina has a free market and almost all foreign currency can be exchanged at down town banks and exchange offices.

The Churches of San Telmo — Due to the proximity to the old port, San Telmo received visitors and sailors from all parts of the world and this explains the numerous churches of different creeds located in the area.

The Danes built their temple on Carlos Calvo 257, a small brick building which, despite its Gothic lines, gets along well with the colonial surroundings.

Another church with nordic reminiscence is the Norwegian, on Ing. Huergo Ave. 126. The author was Alejandro Christophersen, a norwegian himself, who came to Argentina in his early years and was one of the country's most significant architects on account of the quantity and quality of his works.

The Scandinavian trio is completed with the Swedish Church, almost on the border of the neighborhood at 1422 Azopardo St.

• **Russian Orthodox Church**. But those who really deserve a round of applause insofar as religious building is concerned, are the Orthodox Russians, whose main temple we invite you to visit.

This church too was designed by Christophersen, in a style that we could name Russian Bizantine, borrowed from the XVII and XVIII centuries Muscovite churches. The five bulb shaped domes and lobe front are enchanting to be seen through the branches of the trees.

The centralized plant is typical of bizantine architecture, where color and light play a most preponderant role. Don't miss the main altar, with its beautiful icons and religious objects of manificent craftmanship. The paintings on the ceiling, remade not too long ago, when a fire destroyed the original ones, are also worth of attention. They represent figures of the celestial kingdom; their elongated lines, which respond to the bizantine style, are an evident attempt to unify architecture and painting.

Parque Lezama (Lezama Park); Defensa, Brasil, Paseo Colon, Martin Garcia — On this picturesque hill known today as Parque Lezama many historians agree that the first foundation of Buenos Aires took place.

If this is true, Pedro de Mendoza couldn't have picked up a better place, since this small table-land made a perfect lookout to dominate the whole expanse of river (which at that time came right up to the bottom of the hill, now Paseo Colon Avenue).

After various owners, Punta de Santa Catalina (Saint Catherine Point), as it was known then, was bought by the Mackinlays, a young couple who, like other British citizens, had chosen to live in the south. Under the guidance of the Mackinlays, what once had been the first deposit of slaves, leather warehouses and brick ovens, turned into a charming summer residence called by the porteños *La Quinta de los Ingleses* (The English' Summer House).

In 1846, the property was sold to Charles Ridgley Horne, a prosperous American businessman married to an Argentine lady. Horne was responsible for the construction of the house that later would become the National Historic Museum, a mansion that was only paralleled to Rosas residence in the Palermo neighbourhood and was the scene of memorable parties, where all the celebrities of Argentine's past were sure to be present.

The last owner of the house was Jose Gregorio Lezama, who finished off the job in princely style. Lezama had exotic trees planted, fountains and artificial ponds built, gracious stairways constructed, statues and vases distributed around the grounds. And what used to be a semi-wild hill became the most beautiful private park in B.A.

Monument to Pedro de Mendoza
At the entrance to the Lezama Park
(Brasil and Defensa St.), it seems
to welcome those who enter.

In 1894, after Lezama's death, his widow donated the property to the municipality, with the sole condition that the park should carry his name. Down came the surrounding fences, an open air theatre is constructed, restaurants and coffee shops are inaugurated, and even a dancing hall and skating ring built. The house becomes the site of the Museum, and for the first time in its life, San Telmo, this most humble neighbourhood, was able to offer a place which for many years was all the fashion amongst the porteño upper classes.

It is worthwhile to recall this historical past and recreate it in your imagination on entering the park, which certainly is not today what it used to be. The sculptures have deteriorated or been replaced by solemnly boring monuments, the artificial ponds have dried up, little is left of that floral exuberance that used to put perfums on the air... But it is precisely this melancholy what impregnates the Lezama Park with an inimitable atmosphere of remembrance and peace.

We suggest you to visit it on a weekday, when it is not crowded; on Sundays it becomes quite hectic and Saturday evenings, in summertime, public concerts take place. Anyhow, whether by night or in sunshine, solitary or crowded, on weekends or weekdays, the Lezama Park will always be one of B.A.'s most seductive corners.

Museo Historico Nacional (National Historical Museum); Defensa 1600 — It might be a coincidence, but to have the museum with the largest collection of mementos of Argentina's history located in the same place where that history is presumed to have started, seems more than curious.

After a modest start, the museum holds now 20,000 pieces chronologically arranged in 32 halls and 3 galleries which enable you to get a good picture of Argentina, from the discovery of America to the beginning of the forties.

A historical museum is... a historical museum in every part of the world, and we don't want to trick you. Like the others, ours consists of an abundant supply of swords, medals, flags, uniforms, decorations, letters, and many etceteras of the sort. However, it also includes some paintings which, insignificant perhaps from an artistic point of view, will help you to trustworthily visualize the most important episodes of our country's formation.

First and foremost, you should see two large oils by Pedro Subercaseaux, very popular among schoolchildren, known as

El Cabildo Abierto del 22 de Mayo (The City Hall Assembly of May 22) and *La primera ejecucion del Himno Nacional* (The first rendering of the National Anthem). By Jose Bouchet, a painter specialized in historical motives, we have a very good image called *La primera misa en Buenos Aires* (The first mass in B.A.), where the artist depicts the desolate porteño territory at the time of the Spanish conquest.

As for the founding itself, we can imagine Juan de Garay on his historical enterprise if we look carefully at the sketch by Jose Moreno Carbonero entitled precisely *Fundacion de Buenos Aires por Juan de Garay* (The founding of B.A. by Juan de Garay).

There is also a collection of portraits that have their importance, since they give a definite face to the blurred and somewhat mystic image that famous people of the past seem to have. Many of these pictures are by Carlos Morel and Fernando Garcia del Molino, Argentina's first professional painters.

Candido Lopez, whose works are exhibited in Hall XXII, is something else all together and deserves a separate paragraph. Lopez was a soldier and a painter who took part in the war against Paraguay, where he lost his right arm. All the same, using his left hand, he made a series of canvases that illustrate the battle-scenes he witnessed. Don't think of heroic war sights. Lopez painted in a delightful style, respectful of details and poetic in color, a style that today we could call naif although at his time his work was appreciated only as an accurate piece of graphic chronicle. And yet, as contemporary critics have understood, Candido Lopez was a true artist and his works we highly recommend.

But probably, what you are most interested in is the spirit of the people, the customs and the way of life in the early Buenos Aires. To get at that, you have a collection of engravings and lithographies by Hipolito Bacle that will clearly show you how the water carrier, the washerwoman or the gaucho —that gaucho who some people are still searching for on Florida St.— looked like.

These works were done by foreigners such as Bacle himself (a Swiss), Palliere, Emeric Essex Vidal, Rugendas, and many others who came here around the mid 1800 and unexpectedly, on coming across the picturesque, the exotic and the romantic that was so much in fashion in Europe, couldn't but leave us these memories, which you shouldn't miss seeing. *Tuesdays to Fridays and Sundays 3 to 7 pm..*

*"Peinetones en la calle" (Hair combs in the street), by Cesar Bacle.
This and other lithographs exhibited in the National Historical Museum
humorously poke fun at the large haircombs that were all
the rage in the Buenos Aires of the past century.*

LA BOCA

If we are to believe the historians, it was here, at the mouth of the Riachuelo (small river) where Pedro de Mendoza founded the first city of Buenos Aires. Juan de Garay, as we know, established his city further north, and *La Boca del Riachuelo* (the mouth of the small river), later known just plainly as La Boca, an easily flooded lowland, vegetated through years as a no-man's land totally ignored by the settlers of the recently founded metropolis.

It was ignored as a place to live in, but not as a port, which it was and very active indeed. In no time, an ever increasing number of shipyards, naval stores, wool deposits and salting plants established on the banks of the river.

After the fall of Rosas (1852), it was the turn of the immigrants. Greeks, Yugoslavs, Turks, and Italians above all, mainly from Genoa. Arriving by the hundreds, they built there unusual modest wood-framed houses set on piles, with zinc pan-
nels painted no matter which color and often more than one;
the idea was to take advantage of the paint left over from their
boats. A canoe hanging from the door was a clear sign of the
constant threat of floods.

With time, the population grew and the district gained an
identity of its own. It was really a peculiar sailors' village, where
zeneixe —the genoese dialect— often outspoke Spanish; a
high-spirited and boisterous people with tight knitted tradi-
tions; a fraternal community proud of their progress obtained
through tenacity and sacrifice.

1. *Caminito*
2. *Museo de Bellas Artes*
3. *Plaza Solís*
4. *Puente N. Avellaneda*
5. *Puente viejo (de hierro).*

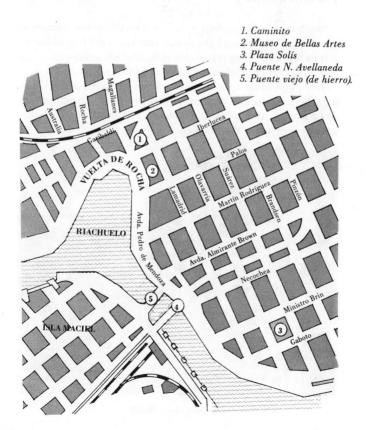

The inhabitants of La Boca had their own newspaper and magazines, they founded theaters and clubs and of course art was never left aside. La Boca even sent the first socialist deputy to parliament (Alfredo Palacios) and, last but not least, they also opened up those famous cantinas where traditional dishes were served to the tune of a tarantella or a nostalgic canzonetta.

In 1882, the zeneixe "nation" decided to declare The Independent Republic of La Boca, Italian flag included. Obviously, they were not taken seriously and the whole thing didn't go beyond an anecdote to smile at, after which La Boca became what it is today, a world of its own, a true city within a city, and one of the most colorful neighborhoods in Buenos Aires.

La Boca today

Such was La Boca. And such it still is. Of course, canoes at the door of the houses have disappeared, but the fear of floods left its mark on queer raised sidewalks that will make your walking a rhythmical and somehow tiring job.

Although some apartment buildings have cropped up here and there —specially on Almirante Brown Ave., the main street in La Boca—, the painted tin houses are likely to appear almost at every corner of the district.

Caminito (Little Road)

The traditional cantinas, packed now along the touristical Necochea St., are not so spontaneously merry as they used to be and cannot hide a suspicious touch *For Export* when a sightseeing bus shows up, but they still will provide those unmatched tasty pastas and shellfish of their motherland.

Probably, what has changed the most in La Boca is the population. When a new port was constructed further north, those hard working Genoese moved off to more comfortable districts and their place was either left vacant or taken up by a different kind of people. The old river bank was marginated from social progress and is today submerged in a sad decadence.

Anyway, La Boca has a lot to offer; but before you start exploring its hidden corners, you'd better get acquainted with the traditional sites that have made this neighborhood famous. Surely, one of these is Caminito.

Caminito (Little Road) — Caminito is simply a street, but a most unusual one indeed. No doors nor entrances of any kind can be seen along it, only a few windows and an occasional balcony or terrace full of colorful plants and flowers. A medium size wall all around its perimeter holds bas-reliefs, paintings, ceramics and other decorations; behind it, the back of the houses show off their typically painted tin walls.

The fact is that Caminito wasn't born a street. It was a detour of the old Ferrocarril Sud (south railway), with time felt into disuse. The neighbors called it *la curva* (the curve) and it was often used by Juan de Dios Filiberto, author of the famous tango Caminito.

After Filiberto's death, artist Benito Quinquela Martin, his close friend, thought it a good idea to name the "little road" after the title of his most popular song. He applied to the municipality, permission was granted, and the curve became officially Caminito Street. The tracks were immediately removed, artists from all over the district contributed their artworks to beautify the recently paved short stretch, the neighbors went out of their way to keep their homes spick-and-span; in short, they all collaborated to turn Caminito into a picturesque outdoor museum and art corner. Furthermore, in summertime an unusual theatre was added that took advantage of the surrounding buildings as a scenery, and these, in turn, were used by their owners as an improvised, comfortable and free of charge theatre box from which the show could be enjoyed.

Museo de Bellas Artes de La Boca (La Boca Fine Arts Museum); 1835 Pedro de Mendoza Ave. — This museum owes its existence to Benito Quinquela Martin, who donated the property not only for that purpose but also for a school whose classrooms he personally decorated. Probably La Boca's greatest benefactor, Quinquela's name is a symbol of the neighborhood.

With the creation of the museum, he established that only works by Argentine artists depicting national reality in figurative lines would be exhibited.

Top level artists such as Lino Spilimbergo, Fortunato Lacamera, Juan Carlos Castagnino, Fernando Fader, Pio Collivadino among many others, can be seen. As for Quinquela's work, you can appreciate it on the last floor of the house, where the artist lived to his last days.

Sculpture is also well represented by artists such as Zonza Briano, Alberto Lagos and Rogelio Yrurtia, exhibited on three beautiful terraces that lead the way to the Teatro de la Ribera, another of Quinquela's donations.

We suggest you don't overlook Room 2, where an unusual collection of nautical prow figureheads are displayed. *Every day 9 am. to 6 pm.*

The neighborhood — If you are trying to get the most out of La Boca, the real jewels of this tour are undoubtedly the streets.

A suggested itinerary might start at Garibaldi St., which you'll find at the end of Caminito turning left. You will notice that the old narrow railway tracks are still there, "bordered with clovers and flowered weeds" (as the tango goes). To one side and the other of the road, the typical tin houses can be seen, and also now and then a brick one which in the general context seems even luxurious, the whole in a peaceful atmosphere that has made many artists set up their ateliers here.

On reaching Rocha or Australia streets, you can turn left, and a few steps ahead you'll find Pedro de Mendoza Ave. Following it north you'll come to the Vuelta de Rocha, that is, the legendary port where La Boca was born. There is no need we advise you to look at the abandoned old vessels dying away in the water and sun, but do take your time to *sense* the grey color of the scenery and compare it with the bright yellows and greens of Garibaldi St. or the colorful Caminito.

Most of the streets in La Boca end their run at this river bank;

going up anyone of them will take you to a strange and bustling world, where the sordid and the picturesque go hand in hand with the historical.

A tin house in La Boca.
Probably the most picturesque architecture in B.A.
Note the steps which raise the level of the sidewalk.

At 567 Brandsen St. you'll find the headquarters of La Boca Volunteer Firemen, one of the first institutions created for the benefit of the neighborhood. They still conserve an old horse-drawn fire wagon, totally made out of bronze, with a steam engine in perfect working conditions. The corner of Brandsen and Necochea is also of historical value, since it was there that Juan de Dios Filiberto was born; and while we're talking of tango, don't miss the corner of Suarez and Necochea, where that "shocking affair" called tango was first danced before it was finally accepted by *decent* families. A bit further on, and still on Suarez St., you'll reach Plaza Solis, La Boca's first public park. Ancient typical houses, naval supply shops and sailors' cafes still can be seen on the bordering streets. The market on Olavarria and Ministro Brin is at least 100 years old and still going strong. Palos 460 (just a little further away) treasures an old building that has become a large tenement house hosting at least thirty families; its huge patio was often used by movie makers when local color scenes were required.

And so on. Many other interesting houses and corners in La Boca will guide your walking and catch your eye, but the pleasure to casually discover the whole thing is yours.

Now, if you really wish to make an overall sightseeing of La Boca, you should cross the river and reach a place called **Isla Maciel** (Maciel Island). To get there you have frequent boat service from the pier near the old bridge (iron structure). The waters of the Riachuelo are not exactly crystalline and you won't find a paradise at the Isla Maciel, but the experience is worthwhile for the hunting-type tourist. (No cameras, of course, and watch your wallet).

On the way back, from the top of the modern Avellaneda Bridge you can afford a breathtaking panoramic view of the site.

WHERE TO EAT IN THIS AREA

CASA DEL ATUN - Almirante Brown 1127
IL CASTELLO - Pedro de Mendoza 1455
IL PICCOLO NAVIO - Necochea 1190
SPADAVECCHIA - Necochea 1180

Nicolas Avellaneda Bridge
Keypoint of La Boca which links Buenos Aires with
the Maciel Island, situated on the other side of the Riachuelo.

This small boat is for no romantic cruise.
It is used to ferry passengers across the Riachuelo.
Luckily enough, it is a short trip...

COSTANERA SUR

After so many stories of floods and other aquatic calamities, you must be wondering where the river, that famous widest river in the world, is. A city born "to open doors to the land", has it no port, no beach, no riverside drive? To answer these and other questions, we invite you on a tour that will prove one of the most interesting in B.A.

From the corner of Paseo Colon and Belgrano Ave, proceeding eastwards along the latter you'll soon come across a series of old bridges, canals, cargo wagons, cranes and other elements characteristic of a port infrastructure.

In fact, you have entered Puerto Madero, one of B.A.'s three ports. Puerto Madero was constructed with lack of foresight and in no time became obsolete, so that Puerto Nuevo (New Port) had to be built in the area behind Retiro.

Not only did this determine a waste of money; from an urbanistic point of view, the worst of it was that, with the construc-

Madero Port.
Aerial view of the huge area which deprived B.A. of its river.

tion of the port, a curtain was drawn between the city and its river and B.A. lost that endless expanse of water which had always been an inseparable feature in its landscape.

This problem was in great measure corrected with the opening of the Avenida Costanera (South Riverside), to which you'll get after crossing the zone just described.

From the very moment it was inaugurated, in November 1918, the Costanera became one of the city's most popular places. Bordered by gardens and green open spaces, it was really a superb promenade. Alongside the river was the so called *rambla* (broadwalk), formed by three consecutive avenues: Martin Noel, Tristan Achaval, and España, giving way to a bathing resort with 250 cabins and steps that led down to the water. There was also a pier for fishermen and a romantic belle-epoque pergola. Inland, along Av. de los Italianos, tea shops, cafes, restaurants and beer houses sprung up like mushrooms. All in all, a playground thought up for everybody, pedestrians and motorists, young and old, rich and poor, people who comfortably could reach it from the same spot where we shall now start our tour: the corner of Belgrano and Av. de los Italianos.

Whether you choose to turn right or left, you'll surely be surprised by its solitary atmosphere. And yet, the place is charming. Towards the north, that means to your left, you will see carefully kept carpets of grass that lead to what used to be the Munich Beer House, in its time the most élite place of the Costanera. The Munich no longer exists as such, but in its place an interesting museum can be found.

• **Museo de Telecomunicaciones** (Telecommunications Museum); Av. de los Italianos 857 — It is worthwhile visiting this museum, didactical and very well organized. Here you'll be able to see the primitive telephone sets alongside with the most sophisticated and modern equipment. Transparent phones enable the observer to study their mechanism, and many devices can be freely operated by the public —something quite unusual in a museum and certainly a lot of fun. *Thursdays through Sundays, 5 to 9 pm. in summer; 3 to 7 pm. in winter.*

• Further on you'll find Darsena Norte, ending point of the Costanera Sur, where the **Buque Museo Fragata Sarmiento** (Frigate Sarmiento Museum) is anchored. This ship served for more than 37 years as a training school for naval cadets; if you are a lover of the seas you shouldn't miss visiting it. *Saturdays and Sundays 2 to 7.30 pm.*

Sarmiento Frigate.
After 39 trips around the world it has retired,
but it still is luxuriant, appealing and loved by the porteños.

To the south the Costanera becomes more solitary, even more desolate, almost an archeological expedition that makes it all the more interesting. A restaurant or a pub now and then, seem to be there only to remind you of past splendors, but more eloquent still is to suddenly come across with splendid buildings now in ruins which today are only tramps' shelters or improvised storehouses.

And then suddenly, a comforting sight: the Fuente de las Nereidas, by Argentine sculptress Lola Mora.

• **Fuente de las Nereidas** (Fountain of the Sea Nymphs) — Not many people are acquainted with this name, given to the fountain by the artist herself; in fact it has always been known as *La Fuente de Lora Mora* (Lola Mora's Fountain) since it arised more attention that the author were a woman than the artistic beauty of the work.

The fountain has a classic pyramidal symmetry, although mannierism can be clearly seen in the twisting of the figures; a baroque influence is also noticeable in the dynamism of the forms and the subtle sensuality which emanates from the whole composition. As it was to be expected, Lola Mora was criticized on account of the great number of nudes displayed and specially for their being so near to the Cathedral, which was the original site of the fountain. But in the long run, as it happened to other controversial pieces of art in B.A., this one too was relocated, at the same place where it stands today.

"Nereidas Fountain", by Lola Mora.

• **Museo de Calcos y Escultura Comparada** (Reproductions and Comparative Sculpture Museum); Gaspar Melchor de Jovellanos 1701) — On the corner of the riverside drive and Brasil Ave. you will find the entrance to this interesting two-hall museum, literally packed with an amazing collection of universal sculpture in excellent plaster reproductions.

From the Louvre, the British Museum and other important museums of the world, they entered Buenos Aires during the twenties. However, owing to some mysterious reason they were kept away for many years in different warehouses of the city and even in unimaginable places like the Water Works Building, where quartered troops used them in their target shooting exercises.

With such a background it is almost a miracle that more pieces were not lost than those which actually did disappear. Still today the exact number of works arrived is unknown, but somewhere between 500 and 2000 is the estimated figure. Around 500 of these were rescued by Argentine painter Ernesto de la Carcova and today they make up this unusual museum, the only one of its kind in Latin America. A visit to it is naturally a must. *Mondays through Fridays 9 to 12 am.; Saturdays and Sundays from 11 am. to 6 pm.*

The river — Although Av. de los Italianos is no doubt a beautiful corner, the Telecommunications Museum a more than didactical entertainment, and you've surely found the Lola Mora Fountain utterly fascinating, you came to the Costanera to see the river and nothing else.

Well, the time has come to tell you the truth: the river no longer exists, it's gone, it has disappeared. But we also want to tell you how and why it happened.

At the beginning of the fifties, B.A. started to gain a more sophisticated look and the Costanera declined as an entertainment and elegance center. Cafes and restaurants moved north, beaches and resorts followed suit, and of course people in droves chose the same area, leaving behind the spot that for more than 30 years had incorporated the river into the everyday life of the porteños.

With this human desertion, the area fell into abandonment, garbage accumulated, the waters became poluted, decay set in... and the Costanera turned into a sorrowful ruin.

Some fifteen years ago, the then Mayor thought it a bright idea to enlarge the city by borrowing space from the river —

as if B.A. really needed to!— and a short while later endless lines of trucks could be seen unloading earth and rubble into our long suffered river, that slowly began to disappear from sight.

But, can a river disappear? Of course not.

With time, the filling project was filed, but the huge quantity of material deposited there gave way to the formation of an artificial island. In this island, vegetation spontaneously flourished and, with it, more than 140 animal species deprived of their natural habitat probably since the Spaniards set foot on these shores.

What was there to do with these unexpected visitors? The answer was obvious: a natural reserve. The project is already under way, along with an integral plan for the recuperation of the riverside; meanwhile, guided tours are making available for schoolchildren and public in general the fun of getting acquainted with our fauna and flora, in a spot that is no doubt a most unusual urban landscape.

And all that, just a few steps away from Plaza de Mayo.

Saturdays and Sundays from 2 pm. on. Additional information can be obtained at 30-3778 and 331-4864.

HOW TO GET THERE

Buses: Lines 2, 9, 10, 25, 28, 29, 33, 46, 53, 54, 61, 64, 86, 93, 126, 143, 152, 159.

Plaza de la República
The obelisk, of course. And also part of the huge 9 de Julio Ave.

Tour 5

Plaza de la Republica
Plaza Lavalle

Unlike other zones of the city, that reach their climax at some special time of the day, Plaza de la Republica is day and night in full swing. Movie, theatre, pizza, books, could all be a good synthesis to define the area.

Lavalle Square, more hectic during the day, turns magically special at night, surely due to the proximity of the Colon Theatre or the Cervantes. Art and culture could be another good synthesis for it.

Inasmuch as synthesis always seem to rob a large portion of reality, in order to have a true picture of the spot, let's get to know its landmarks and above all its history.

PLAZA DE LA REPUBLICA

This is a plaza with no past, simply because it was never a plaza, nor a dump, nor a halting place for carts, nor a manor house, nor in fact any of those ancestors that gave way to other squares in Buenos Aires. Plaza de la Republica is just a cross-roads, a rond-point.

In order to exist at all, it had to do away with hundreds of buildings, and of course to put up with the protest of neighbors who considered that their rights had been violated. Progress was under way...

It was then 1936 and B.A. was growing at full speed, opening up avenues, erecting buildings, multiplying its transport services, planting statues and monuments all over the place.

Corrientes St., just like any other, felt the impact. To make

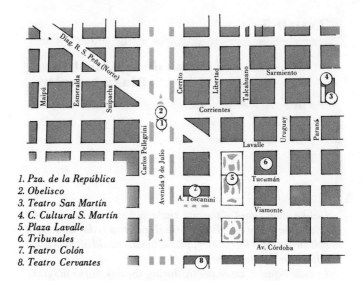

1. Pza. de la República
2. Obelisco
3. Teatro San Martín
4. C. Cultural S. Martín
5. Plaza Lavalle
6. Tribunales
7. Teatro Colón
8. Teatro Cervantes

way for the cabarets, bookstores and cafes which had over-crowded its narrow sidewalks, it had to be widened. Perpendic-ular to Corrientes, another great avenue was coming to life: 9 de Julio, whose enormous span of 140 m across, made it the widest in the world.

At the crossing of the two avenues, a huge empty space appeared. What should be done with it? How could this no-man's land be organized into a proper circulating area for the 40,000 cars which at that time were driving by?

That's how Plaza de la Republica was born. A product of the offspring of the XX century and its urbanistic demands, with no venerable past, surrounded by night life and bohemian folk.

Plaza de la Republica today

As time went by, Plaza de la Republica became the heart of Buenos Aires. Center of show business and recognizable point of reference for residents and tourists alike, favorite spot for every popular celebration... And with a monument right in the middle of it which you must already be wondering about: the obelisk.

The obelisk — On March 23rd, 1936, the same year in which the widening of Corrientes was concluded, the obelisk was inaugurated on the Plaza de la Republica in commemoration of the fourth centenary of B.A.'s first foundation.

It was designed by architect Alberto Prebish, who conceived a concrete structure 67 m high, at whose top a lightning rod was placed. To reach this point, a 200 step ladder was built inside the monument, and whoever wanted to climb it, was rewarded with a wonderful bird's eyeview of the city —although the spot could also be occasionally chosen as a suicidal diving board, as was the case with a jobless porteño that has already entered into the legend.

Of course, that didn't happen very often, but it can't be said that the obelisk had an easy life. The same as the Eiffel Tower in Paris, our monument has been widely criticized because it supposedly spoiled the beauty of the city. Today, 51 years later, that "ridiculous nonsense", that "paper sticker" which was on the verge of being torn down altogether "for the sake of esthetics and public security", has definitely won the heart of the porteños and triumphantly rises in the middle of the most popular corner of B.A., as one of its unavoidable features.

Corrientes Avenue — Three avenues cross Plaza de la Republica: Nueve de Julio, Diagonal Norte (R.S. Peña Ave.) and Corrientes. All three date back to the thirties, but whilst the first two were born, so to speak, already adult, Corrientes grew up hand on hand with the city.

It was narrow, like all the streets in the old B.A.. But suddenly, when the explosion of progress took place, it started gaining importance. The best theatres settled on its sidewalks; restaurants, bars and pizza parlors were insufficient for the increasing crowds; bookstores open all night long gave the porteños the key to culture.

Frenzy was at its topmost during the mad twenties, and with the invasion of automobiles the situation grew to proportions that could barely be handled.

Corrientes had to be widened. More than 100 years after Pres. Rivadavia's visionary urban plan, back in 1822, and to the dismay of the traditionalist groups afraid of losing their cultural and recreational center.

With time, Corrientes had competitors. Lavalle street took over most of the movies, while off Corrientes shows moved to San Telmo, and so did tango bars and modern cafes-concert.

Nevertheless, "the street that never sleeps", as someone called it, never betrayed its destiny and much of its essence can still be savoured, especially at night on the sector stretching from the obelisk to Callao. Along these seven blocks, you'll want to visit the oldest cafes and watch their customers; it will be wonderful fun to browse through the second-hand bookstores; you will get to discover, along with the first line cinemas, that small camouflaged hall in some cellar or gallery... and so many other things of the old times that haven't at all quite gone off.

Teatro General San Martin (General San Martin Theatre); Corrientes 1530 — Corrientes surely brings out a nostalgic feeling, but in no way melancholy. Proving that life prevails over death is this imposing structure known as Teatro General San Martin. Designed by the architect Mario Roberto Alvarez, the building, inaugurated in 1961, hosts in its 13 floors: five theatre stages, two museums, art galleries, auditoriums, accomodation for international symposiums, and everything that could be desired in cultural activity.

To be precise, the building you are looking at is part of a complex divided into two independent sectors attending different matters. The sector overlooking Corrientes is devoted to all activities regarding showbusiness; the rest has its own building on Sarmiento 1551.

If you get in through Corrientes you'll have access to several theatre halls. The **Sala Martin Coronado** is the main one, with a seating capacity for 700 people. Its huge stage, the only one in the country as for dimensions and mechanical gadgets, usually stages pieces of great universal and Argentine playwriters. Smaller than the Martin Coronado is the Sala Casacuberta; its semi-circular design, similar to a Greek theatre, turns it into a modern "theatre in the round". On the basement floor is the **Sala Cunil Cabanellas**, reserved for only 200 spectators and the ideal stage for chamber or experimental theatre.

A fourth hall is found on the ground floor. As a matter of fact it is simply a huge space with no seating accomodations, actually robbed from the main hall of the building, where the audience can sit on the floor, on the stairs, or wherever they like, and enjoy free of charge shows, usually musical. Of course these performances are very representative of the spirit of Corrientes, a street which never was of the highbrow type.

Finally, on the 10th floor, is the **Sala Leopoldo Lugones**,

Gral. San Martin Municipal Theater.
Including museums, concert and exhibtion halls.

reserved for collection pictures enjoyed by long lines of mindful adicts to the seventh art.

• **Museo Municipal de Arte Moderno** (Municipal Museum of Modern Art). You'll find it on the 9th and 8th floors. On exhibition are contemporary paintings and sculptures by Pettoruti, Battle Planas, Berni, Raquel Forner, among other great Argentine artists, together with famous universal plastics such as Klee, Mondrian, Vasarely, Matisse... *Tuesdays through Sundays 4 to 8 pm..*

N.B. Very soon this museum will be transfered to its new headquarters at San Juan 350, right in the core of the San Telmo district.

- **Museo Municipal de Artes Plasticas Eduardo Sivori** (Municipal Museum of Plastic Arts Eduardo Sivori). Two floors further down, you'll come across this museum, devoted exclusively to Argentine artists as from the XIX century up to date. (*Tuesdays through Sundays from 4 to 8 pm.*)

- **Photography** is also well represented at the San Martin. Two halls were dedicated to it on the ground floor, forming a gallery which links the Corrientes building with the other sector of the complex.

Centro Cultural San Martin (San Martin Cultural Center); Sarmiento 1551

The most diverse activities take place here. You can choose a conference, a concert or a round table and there is no need worrying about the cost: it's all free of charge.

While you are deciding, let's suggest you stop before two sculptures by Argentine artists worthy your time. One is *Los Acrobatas* (The Acrobats) by Curatella Manes; the other is *Figura Reclinada* (Reclined Figure), a bronze by Naum Knop. Both can be seen on the terrace which gives access into the building.

Lavalle, the street of the movies

On this pedestrian street parallel to Corrientes, you will find the city's major movie district, along an equal number of pizza parlors and bars.

The flow of people is intense and continuous, especially on Saturday nights, when the crowds are quite overwhelming. It is actually a good sign of the prevailing spirit in the area, where everybody wants to get away from it all.

> *In the last few years a new and exclusive movie district has appeared in the area surrounding Santa Fe and Callao Avenues. These theatres are a bit more expensive than those located on Lavalle St., but the zone is worthwhile the difference.*

San Martin Cultural Center.
This section of the San Martin complex has become
the meeting place for crowds of culture hunting public.

PLAZA LAVALLE

Taking Plaza de la Republica as a reference point, if you walk towards the northeast along R.S. Peña Ave, after only 100 meters you'll reach Plaza Lavalle, three blocks limited by Libertad, Cordoba, Talcahuano and Lavalle streets.

How it was

Seeing Plaza Lavalle today, it is hard to believe that not too long ago there was here a low swampy land crossed by a constantly overflowing stream.

A few precarious huts and a modest gun factory amidst bad smelling marshes were not much of an incentive to uproot the porteño families from their traditional habitat at Plaza de Mayo and its surroundings.

Nevertheless, an enterprising group of neighbors decided in 1827 to improve the area by means of a public garden similar to those which at the time were successful in Europe. It was called Parque Argentino —or Vauxhall, after its British homologous—, where tearooms and hotels were built and open air concerts and dances took place.

But the destructive force of nature would get the better part; the stream kept overflowing, taking advantage of most of the improvements, many lots were sold and others simply abandoned.

Anyway, Plaza Lavalle —or Plaza del Parque (Park Plaza), as it was known then— had been born to greater things. In 1857, the leap to the future came with the railroad —the legendary Western Line—, whose terminal station was built on the site occupied today by the Colon Theatre.

Trains left from Park Station, crossed the square alongside Tribunales (Law Courts), headed up Lavalle and on reaching Callao made a left turn towards Corrientes; then Pueyrredon, Bme. Mitre, till they got to Plaza Once, where the terminal is located nowadays. The 'S' shape of **Pasaje Rauch** (between Callao and Rio Bamba) stands as a trace of that initial run.

Whoever says railroad, says progress. Houses started cropping up close to the station, regular transport lines linked the

Lavalle Park. Fountain of the Dancers.
It pays hommage to a ballet corps
tragically killed in a plane crash.

square with different points of the city, and even running water reached the district, a luxury which only a few places in B.A. could at that time boast about.

When the square became too central a place, paradoxically the station had to disappear and the obsolete Gunnery Park followed on. Furthermore, while Alvear was mayor of the city, a final solution to the flowings was found which gave way to the stone paving of the streets and other important urbanistic improvements.

Architectonically, the area started to gain relevance and very soon it became a coveted residential district.

A modern skyscraper in 9 de Julio Avenue.
Situated in front of the Colon Theater (on the left),
they get along amicably with no style rivalry.

How it is

Plaza Lavalle obtained its present outlook with the demolition of the Miro Palace and the construction of the Colon Theatre and the Law Courts, inaugurated in 1908 and 1910 respectively.

The Miro Palace was built in 1868, during the district's urbanistic upheaval, and occupied the block limited by Libertad, Viamonte, Talcahuano and Cordoba St. It was one of B.A.'s prides until 1937, when it was torn down and the land incorporated to Plaza Lavalle. Fortunately, many of the fine trees that surrounded the mansion were saved, so that this block is today not only the most beautiful section of the area, but also a haven of peace in comparison with the bustle of the other two.

Palacio de Justicia (Tribunales) (Law Courts); Talcahuano 550 — In times gone by, lawyers used to carry out their activities under the arches of the Cabildo, which was also the building that housed the prison, the police station and the morgue. As the city grew, and a more appropriate place was needed, the vacant lot left by the Gunnery Park was chosen to erect the monumental building known today as Tribunales (Law Courts), which occupies the whole block surrounded by Talcahuano, Lavalle, Uruguay and Tucuman.

The Law Courts were constructed by Norbert Maillart or Maillard, who shouldn't be misunderstood as Robert Maillart, the swiss engineer who around the same period was revolutionizing his country with his bridges of advanced design.

WHERE TO EAT IN THIS AREA

CARABELAS - Pasaje Carabelas 259
CHIQUIN - Cangallo (now Pres. Peron) 920
EDELWEISS - Libertad 432
EL CIERVO - Callao y Corrientes
LA EMILIANA - Corrientes 1443
LA ESTANCIA - Lavalle 941
LA ONDA VERDE - Corrientes 1580
LOS INMORTALES - Corrientes 1369/Lavalle 746
PIPPO - Montevideo 341
PIZZA HUT - Lavalle 876

This had to be made clear because the building you are facing is far from being avant-guard architecture. The Courts were built when in B.A. eclecticism was in fashion, a style which produced some excellent works but had also a risky trend towards grandiloquence and lack of clearness.

A prestigious Argentine architect said that "the absolute ugliness of Tribunales is difficult to surpass". He surely must be right, but please don't be scared by such a drastic judgement and do visit Plaza Lavalle. It is true that our Law Courts are no model of style, but they still provide a good frame to the plaza and a special atmosphere to the whole area which is now inseparable from it.

The bookstands — If you are interested in these questions about art or in any others, try the second-hand bookstands on Plaza Lavalle, just opposite Tribunales. This open air market, undoubtedly one of the plaza's more typical attractions, was formerly located on the steps of the Cabildo, but had to leave the spot when the latter was remodelled. Now, lawyers and booksellers are once again together.

The Law Courts (Tribunales)
Some architects disagree with the architectural concept.
From the top of his column, Lavalle seems to approve
looking the other way around.

Teatro Colon(Colon Theatre); Libertad 600 — Until 1888 the theatre was located at the corner of Rivadavia and Reconquista, where the Banco de la Nacion (National Bank) stands today. It was an excellent and comfortable building with outstanding technical facilities for such a modest town as B.A. was at that time. However, since by the end of the century it no longer was that modest, a move was considered necessary. The vacant property left by the Railroad Park Station was chosen and the arch. Francisco Tamburini, who had been responsible for the remodelling of the Government House, commissioned for the job.

Tamburini went no further than the blue prints before he died. His successor, Victor Meano, died too before ending his work. It was under the guidance of Belgium arch. Julio Dormal, a resident in Argentina, that the theatre was finished and on May 25th 1908, inaugurated.

There is no way the tourist can miss the Colon Theatre, since it is one of the few historical buildings that has not been smothered by later constructions. Quite the contrary, the opening of 9 de Julio Ave. gave it a greater breathing space on Cerrito St., while a generous free area around its other three sides enables the passerby to appreciate the construction from any possible angle.

The Colon Theatre
The sober Italian lines of the building
burst into an opulent French decor at the interior.

The building is made up of two bodies, the first corresponding to the foyer and the other to the concert hall itself. The facades have also been clearly designed. A sober ground floor becomes more emphatical on reaching the main one; then comes the attic with eyelet windows and carved panels; finally, a simple crowning marks the summit of this noble building, framed in the italianizing esthetics in which its first two architects conceived it.

Typically Italian is also the horseshoe shape of the hall, a design imposed by the great european theatres as the most adequate for a perfect acoustics. And the acoustics of the Colon is really saying something. As many internationally renowned singers have attested, our maximum coliseum is one of the best in the world from that point of view, although an oversized theatre is usually a handicap to a good hearing. The Colon, on the contrary, even if it seats 3,500 spectators —4,000 taking into account those standing— offers perfect sound up to those in the gods, who can pick up the slightest whisper on the stage, seven stories below.

In the foyer, it is the French esthetics which rules indisputed. The White and Golden Halls will surely bring back memories of the Versailles and Schönbrunn Palaces to those who have been there. Don't miss either the **Museum**, where

The Colon Theatre
The facade looking onto Viamonte St. offers enough
space around it, allowing a worthwhile perspective.

The Colon Theatre
Notice the horseshoe shape of the hall, wich offers excellent acoustics.

you'll find an interesting collection of ancient instruments, photographs and other documents related to such artists as Caruso, Toscanini, the Lerner Quartet, Maria Callas, Yehudi Menuhim, the Concertgebouw Orchestra, Placido Domingo and many others that have performed in the Colon throughout its 80 years of life. (*Mondays through Fridays from 12 to 6 p.m.; entrance Tucuman 1161*).

Back in the hall, take time to watch the magnificent chandelier, seven meters in diameter, as well as the paintings of the dome, made by Argentine artist Raul Soldi to replace the original decoration, deteriorated because of a Carnival. Yes, a Carnival. Incredible as it may seem, in 1936 and 1937 carnival was celebrated in this theatre and to make the hot B.A. night a bit more comfortable, an ingenious form of air conditioning was devised. It consisted of ice bars piled on top of the dome which, on melting, spilt cold water through the radiators. The system worked and the dancers survived, but not so the paintings on the inner side of the dome. Anyhow, it was a fortunate misfortune and nothing was really lost. In fact quite the opposite, and the Colon is well off with Soldi's work.

The Colon Theatre
A section of the orchestra seats and boxes during a performance.

Last but not least, the backstage workshops are worth a visit. To get to know them we suggest you arrange a guided tour which will certainly prove a fascinating experience.

If you're in town during the summer, don't miss the outdoors concerts held at Parque Lezama, Recoleta, and Parque Centenario. These are some of the best performances Buenos Aires has to offer and admittance is free.

Teatro Nacional Cervantes (Cervantes National Theatre); Cordoba and Libertad — This is one of the principal stages in Buenos Aires, where the National Company has its headquarters. However, neither the theatre's name nor the style of the building have, as might be expected, any relation with a purely Argentine cultural past. On the contrary, an aggressive Spanish look imposes over you right from the entrance. The facade is borrowed from that of the University of Alcala de Henares, in Spain. Inside, you'll note glazed tiles brought from

Valencia and Seville, tapestries from the Royal Tapestry Mill of Madrid, wrought iron railings copied from El Greco's house in Toledo. Even the seating accomodations are monk style chairs instead of the customary fauteuils.

Such a remarkable building was donated by a great Spanish actress called Maria Guerrero, who wanted in this way to show her gratitude towards B.A. and its people. Today, the theatre stands as one of the best in the city.

HOW TO GET THERE

Subway: Line B - CARLOS PELLEGRINI or
URUGUAY stations.
Line C - LAVALLE or DIAGONAL
NORTE stations.
Line D - 9 DE JULIO or TRIBUNALES
stations.

Buses: Lines 5, 6, 23, 24, 29, 38, 39, 50, 102, 109, 115, 155.

Tour 6

It is rather difficult to give an accurate synthesis of a district where life and death go hand in hand, where art and nature get along amicably, where a high-class neighborhood wholeheart-edly stands the crowds that are increasingly invading all its corners.

Recoleta is just that, a cluster of possibilities, a high voltage tourist attraction where art and history, luxury and entertain-ment get together under the strict code of a high standard of living.

A little history

A glimpse at any map of Buenos Aires will show you that Recoleta was an outskirt, which in the old times meant a deso-late place on the river bank, rich in trees and ditches, idlers and rovers.

To these inhospitable lands came the Recoleto Friars at the beginning of the XVIII century. Economically helped by Juan de Narbona, a picturesque mixture of merchant and smuggler, the Recoletos started the construction of their convent, that was finished in 1732. The church was put under the advocation of the Virgin of the Pilar, but people began to call it Church of the Recoletos or simply La Recoleta, and this name finally was given to the whole surroundings.

Owing to the order's habits of austerity and reclusion, the temple was never very appealing for people to settle in the area. Except for a small plaza before the church and the opening of the Calle Larga (Long Road), today known as Av. Quintana, the Recoleta stuck to its rural characteristics for nearly a century.

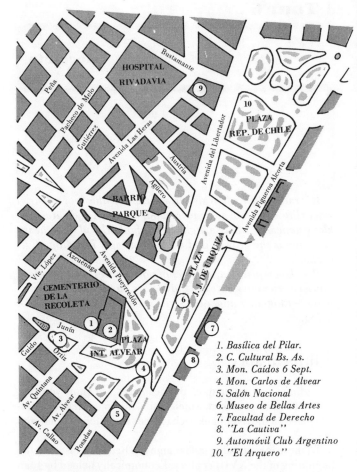

1. Basílica del Pilar.
2. C. Cultural Bs. As.
3. Mon. Caídos 6 Sept.
4. Mon. Carlos de Alvear
5. Salón Nacional
6. Museo de Bellas Artes
7. Facultad de Derecho
8. "La Cautiva"
9. Automóvil Club Argentino
10. "El Arquero"

In 1822, when the order was dissolved, the convent's orchard became a public cemetery —the first in B.A.— and, ironically enough, this place destined to the dead would also become an attraction for those alive.

There was already at that time two yearly pilgrimages, but their popularity increased from that date on. Unfortunately, those meetings usually turned into wild parties which more than once ended in knife duels and crime.

As in other cases, it was Mayor Torcuato de Alvear who once again would put an end to that state of things. The pilgrimages suppressed, radical improvements were made in the cemetery and the plaza that today is called after him. Streets were opened up and luxurious residences constructed, many of which still stand today and others have been replaced by modern towers and hotels.

With time, Recoleta became the neighborhood of the porte-ño élite, a privilege which it retains to this day.

Recoleta today

Apparently, Recoleta has not changed. The essence of the district lies untouched in its illustrious mansions and modern skyscrapers, in the beauty of its parks with their now centennial trees, its wide avenues, its expensive boutiques.

And yet, a metamorphosis at first almost imperceptible is now aggressively changing the spirit of what used to be one of the most exclusive quarters in B.A.

Recoleta was known for its quiet and peaceful streets. Strolling along them was like trespassing a forbidden land where you felt a stranger in an environment to which you didn't belong. But one day in the early fifties, a group of car-races fans —those were Fangio's days— got into the habit of meeting at an anonymous cafe on the corner of Junin and Av. Quintana. It was called Aerobar or La Veredita (nobody really knows any longer), and would later change its name to La Biela (The Rod).

In no time La Biela had its clientele tripled and, what is more, became the place to gather over a cup of coffee, enjoying the peaceful surroundings. As a result, a nearly ignored urban area was rediscovered. People found out that the Pilar church was a colonial relic and not just the church were the wealthy were married; that the cemetery, apart from its illustrious dwellers, held unvaluable artworks and historical memories; that the trees on the plaza were a hundred years and even four centuries old; that the old convent, by then an asylum for the elderly, was a good setting for a museum.

All this was discovered only some years ago. And with the discovery, the peaceful hours were gone and a frenzy era started which doesn't look as though it is ever going to stop.

La Biela soon had company. Classy restaurants and sophisticated cafes sprouted like mushrooms along Junin and R. M. Ortiz streets, competing with each other to seduce an heterogeneous public mindless of age or social standing, whose only aim was to have a good time at the spot which was all the rage.

Faculty of Law.
The elegant colonnade doesn't seem to clash
with the chaotic traffic of the avenue at its feet.

Avenida del Libertador
in the proximity of the Recoleta neighborhood.

The flow of people made it necessary to build underground parking lots. With the plaza turned into a traffic-free area, restaurants and cafés took their tables out into the open and the whole place became a huge colorful terrace surrounded by flowers and roofed with centenary trees.

When the artisans and street artists realized that the zone was being flooded with well-to-do people, they quickly set up their stalls on the slope, openly displaying their merchandise and performing their acts.

And so on. Now we suggest you take a seat at any of the comfortable cafes facing the square and, while you watch the world go by, decide about your next tour and the beautiful things you're going to see in Recoleta.

Basilica del Pilar (Pilar Basilica); Junin 1904 — The best view of the church of Pilar is obtained from Av. Quintana, whence you'll be able to see it neatly outlined against the sky, free of any obstacle.

A first glance shows that the building is divided in four sectors: the main body, a small protruding portico, the bell tower, and the espadaña (a particular kind of belfry). Asymmetric as to size and proportions, these four sectors are visually merged because of their white and yellow color.

The **tower** detaches from the rest on account of its great height. At one time it was the highest point in B.A. and served as the city's lighthouse. Out on the porch, a majolica depicts what the church looked like from the river at the end of the XVIII century. Nowadays, that record has of course been beaten and the most conspicuous feature of the tower is its original bell shaped top, covered with blue and white tiles. Tiles were not typical of colonial architecture, as might be presumed considering that this church is one of the oldest in the city. Not only was B.A. too poor to afford such a luxury, but glazed tiles were introduced in the country only in the XIX century, after the Independence. Those you can see now were added in 1860, when the church was remodelled; moreover, they are of French and not Sevilian origin.

At the right end of the facade, the **espadaña** is another important element to be looked at. An espadaña is simply a hollow belfry, which enables the bells to be freely seen. This one is double arched and holds a quite original clock whose face and dials have been traced upon a ball of masonry. In spite of its age, it still works perfectly well.

No matter how glamourous the outside may seem, the best of the Pilar church is found inside.

After passing the wooden doors with ancient ironwork, you'll be able to walk down the only nave, bordered by six chapels which date back to the viceroyal period. They are supposed to be the work of only one artist, probably of portuguese or german origin, judging from their baroque lavish decoration.

Compared with the side chapels, the main altar does not particularly stands out, except for its silver front, that comes from Peru and is thought to be the work of Cuzco indians. In the center of the carving, an Incan sun is clearly outlined.

A life-size image of **San Pedro de Alcantara** is also worthwhile seeing. You'll find it in a chapel on the left at the entrance. It was attributed to Alonso Cano, the great andalusian sculptor, but studies are being made to clear up the question.

To end your visit to the Basilica of the Pilar, take a look to the Altar de las Reliquias (Altar of the Relics), on the right next to the entrance, where the supposed remains of saints and apostles are kept.

Cementerio de La Recoleta (Recoleta's Cemetery);
Junin 1760 — Not always is a cemetery a sullen place. La Recoleta, in fact, has been from its very beginning a cultural event.

The North Cemetery, as it was called in the past, was created to end with that old tradition of burying the dead in the churches, or around them, or... no matter where, according of course to their social status.

With the creation of a public cemetery, improved sanitary conditions and equal burial treatment were intended, but these goals were only half attained. If the city's salubrity undoubtedly changed for the better, the democratic spirit on the contrary was left aside, since the Recoleta became over the years the most aristocratic burial ground in B.A., exclusive for wealthy families and national outstanding personalities.

However, owing to these circumstances we are today able to admire a rich sculptural complex, that will help you to capture the mentality and tastes of last century's porteños.

It is easy to notice that what abounds in Recoleta are clumsy and bombastic buildings, mournful virgins, madonnas of hyperbolic gestures, giant angels atop pinacles of towering height. Learning shows off in some gothic tombs; in others, snobbery turns to the lines of a greek temple or to the egypti-

Basilica del Pilar
Detail of the espadaña (belfry), a true relic
in one of Buenos Aires oldest churches.

an style, so in fashion during the last century. Something that probably will call your attention are the many torches with up-sidedown flames, which are said to be a masonic sign.

In short, a showroom of the multiplicity of periods, fashions, ideologies, personal whims and, of course, the economical power of those who lie there.

The works are mainly by Italian and French sculptors with excellent craftmanship, who repeat the models of the great artists of the past. Anyhow, amidst the prevailing mediocrity, some pieces outstand because of other values. You'll find them in the area closest to Azcuenaga St. (at the rear of the grounds) and were made by two Argentine artists of this century: Lucio Correa Morales (tombs of Angela Menendez and of Emma

Nicolai de Caprile) and Agustin Riganelli (Rufino de Elizalde's grave). In spite of their modest dimensions, both convey a great spiritual strengh.

• **Monumento a los caídos el 6 de septiembre** (Monument to the fallen on September 6th), by Riganelli. Since this is a funeral monument, it can be considered as part of the cemetery although it is located outside its grounds.

The episode that inspired the work —a military uprising in which many youths lost their lives— was inviting for a grandieloquent conception, so that you'll probably feel a bit disappointed at the simplicity of the sculpture. No trumpeting angels or mythological allegories in here, just a mother and her son lying dead on her lap, a *pietá* in the classical sense of the word. Instead of amazement, it conveys an idea, a thought that can be plainly put in these words: the ultimate consequence of violence is the death of our sons.

Recoleta Cemetery
An art nouveau style sepulcre
one of the most artistic in the necropolis.

Centro Cultural de Buenos Aires (Buenos Aires Cultural Center); Junin 1930 — Up to not too long ago there was here a shadowy brick wall that enclosed what used to be the old Recoleto convent and later a hospital, a jail, a fire station and, lastly, an asylum for the elder.

At the turn of this decade it was decided to turn the property into a cultural center, for which three architects were commissioned: Clorindo Testa, Jacques Bedel, and Luis Benedit. The construction is not finished yet, but what has been carried out up to now is an important accomplishment in the field of contemporary art.

The old structures were maintained and new ones were added so that past and present styles are now merged in an original architectonic conception. The cloisters have turned into exhibition galleries keeping their colonial touch, and the same can be said of the orange grove and the Fountain and Linden patios. The old chapel is now an auditorium, where the original doors and stained glass windows have been preserved.

Buenos Aires Cultural Center.
The picture was made when the house was
a home for the elderly.
Notice the solitude of the environment.

The terrace, with its notched walls resembling ruins is one of the most interesting places in the building. The place also affords a panoramic view of the area including the cemetery.

In short, what used to be an old folks home has become a cultural focus, a small Pompidou Center where art and culture have been made available for everybody.

Monument to Gral. Carlos M. de Alvear —

Though somewhat blocked by new buildings, a good view of this monument is obtained from the top of the hill. Its author was great French sculptor Antoine Bourdelle, who spent nearly ten years to finish his work, after going through a long research period and an endless number of sketches and models.

In other words, a total guaranty of professionalism and earnest self criticism. And yet, it is said that when the final draft was presented, the military authorities were reluctant because, according to military rule, a general on horseback must always be represented wearing his cap and Bourdelle's was missing his. When questioned, the artist answered that his general was a hero and had lost his cap in combat. After which... he promptly went back to work.

Before sending the monument to Buenos Aires, it was exhibited in Paris and the French government was so impressed that they were on the verge of declaring it a national patrimony. Fortunately, nothing of the sort happened, the statue arrived to B.A. in 1925, and a year afterwards was happily unveiled.

Salon Nacional de Artes Plasticas (National Hall of Plastic Art) — Behind the Alvear Monument stands the salmon colored building of the National Hall. Time ago it used to be a well known cabaret called Palais de Glace. Today, this flat dome construction houses one of the most important art exhibitions in B.A. If you happen to be in the city when it is held, be sure not to miss it. Entrance is on Posadas 1725.

Museo Nacional de Bellas Artes (The National Fine Arts Museum); Libertador Ave. 1473 — Museums of this sort are in other parts of the world usually set in representative buildings. This is not the case with our Fine Arts Museum, which although being located in an area surrounded by princely mansions, it consists of a simply pink painted box shape construction easily identifiable.

The building was originally a water purifying plant in which the museum was set up after a curious pilgrimage. Its first headquarters had been the Bon Marché, from which several rooms were sort of borrowed (see page   ). In 1910 it was relocated in Plaza San Martin, in a dismountable pavillion that had been used to represent Argentina in the Paris Universal Exhibition of 1889.

In 1931, when the paintings were far too many, it was once again moved, this time to the old Waterworks Building, where it stands today. The building was remodelled by arch. Alejandro Bustillo into nine different halls occupying a surface of nearly 10,000 square meters and almost an equal number of paintings, sculptures, tapestries and etchings.

The collections cover nearly all phases of western art. Middle Ages, Renaissance, XVII and XVIII centuries can be seen in the seven halls of the ground floor. The highlights are Goya, El Greco, Tintoretto, Rubens and Zurbaran, along with valuable wooden carvings of Spanish origin.

Also on the ground floor you'll find XIX century's art. The Impressionists and post-impressionists are represented through the works of Renoir, Toulouse Lautrec, Gauguin, Van Gogh, Degas and many others. There are also 20 sculptures by Rodin (**The Kiss** among others) and works by his disciple Bourdelle.

To see the XX century art, you must go up to the first floor, where paintings by Picasso, Kandinsky, Klee and others can be appreciated. This floor is actually almost exclusively devoted to Argentine artists; a walk through it will be a fine way of getting acquainted with these men who contributed ever so much to national art.

Sculptures, engravings, prints, watercolors and the like add to the Fine Arts Museum patrimony, as well as special exhibitions which bring to Buenos Aires the art of the whole world. *Tuesdays to Saturdays from 9 am. to 1 pm. and 3 pm. to 7 pm.*

Museo Nacional de Arte Decorativo (National Museum of Decorative Art); Av. Libertador 1902 — Unlike the Fine Arts Museum, here the building is in accordance with its interior and prepares you to an encounter with good taste, luxury and elegance.

Built in 1911 for Matias Errazuriz, this beautiful residence by architect René Sergent is a real summary of the French styles going from the Renaissance to the XVIII c. You'll find here a

Renaissance hall, a Louis XIV salon, another of the XVIII century and a Regency hall inspired on the famous Salon Oval of the Parisian Hotel Soubise.

On the first floor, the Sert Salon is an exception. It was decorated by the catalonian painter of that name and displays a Goya like decoration with a flash of the style developed by Leon Bakst in his gorgeous sceneries for Diaghilev's Russian ballets.

National Museum of Decorative Art
Its sumptuous entrance is only an invitation of what is offered inside.
Currently open at the Errazuriz Palace.

A wide assortment of furniture, ceramics, paintings, musical instruments, chandelliers, and other exquisite items will prove a delightful sight to all art collectors.

• **Museo Nacional de Arte Oriental** (National Museum of Oriental Art) — A very complete collection of Near, Middle and Far East art is exhibited in this museum, provisionally open to the public on the second floor of the Errazuriz Palace until its definite site at Callao 628 is finished.

Walking around

— A stroll from the Recoleta to the Decorative Arts Museum will bring you across very interesting argentine and european pieces of sculpture.

On the gardens surrounding the Fine Arts Museum, a metal structure by Enio Iommi whose contemporary lines go along well with the prevailing classicism of the area. Bourdelle is again present in **Hercules Arquero** (Hercules Archer) and **El ultimo centauro** (The Last Centaur).

WHERE TO EAT IN THIS AREA

AU BEC FIN - Vicente Lopez 1825
BRASSERIE LIPP - Ayacucho 2027
CLARK'S I - Junin 1777
DON JUAN - Roberto M. Ortiz 1827
EL CEIBAL - Las Heras 2265
ESTILO MUNICH - Roberto M. Ortiz 1875
GATO DUMAS - Roberto M. Ortiz 1809
HARPER'S - Junin 1763
HIPPOPOTAMUS - Junin 1787
LA STREGA - Ocampo 2556
LA TASCA DEL OSO - Avda. Alvear 1889
LA ZI TERESA DI NAPOLI - Las Heras 2939
LOLA - Roberto M. Ortiz 1805
NORTE - Junin 1767
RINCON DE LOPEZ - Junin 1745
ROBERTINO - Vicente Lopez 2158
TEMPONE'S - Junin 1727
VILLAGE - Junin 1735

Another interesting piece is **La Cautiva**, by Lucio Correa Morales, which you'll find to the south of the School of Law, on the corner of Fig. Alcorta and Pueyrredon Avenues; it represents the situation of the indians at the start of the century, in danger of being wiped off because of the social changes. An indian woman "is sitting on the ruins of a wall, looking on into the distance in search of the camp site she will never see again. Her children are hiding like frightened baby chicks, while the dog is there to follow the long trail of captives...". The description belongs to Correa Morales himself.

This neighborhood close to Av. del Libertador
has beautiful hidden corners such as the one
that can be seen in the picture.

The Belgian Constantin Meunier is another great artist whose works adorn the greenery surrounding the Fine Arts Museum. **El Sembrador** and **El Segador** (The Sower and The Reaper), two vigorous figures representing hand labourers, denounce the artist's debt to the realism started by Courbet. You'll find these sculptures at the farthest end of the Museum, on Plaza Justo J. de Urquiza.

The work of a fellow countryman, Alberto Lagos, can be seen at Plaza Rep. de Chile, on the corner of Bustamante and Av. Libertador, in front of the Decorative Art Museum. His **Arquero de San Sebastian** (The Archer of St. Sebastian) flaunts an athletic figure surrounded by the trees which, on being viewed, is a true feast.

As a matter of fact, everything in Recoleta is a feast. It is more than evident that we are in a zone where good living is the word. Lavishly sumptuous buildings, patrician residences, gardens and parks is what you'll enjoy if you return to the starting point of this tour by bordering Av. del Libertador and Av. Fig. Alcorta. And don't overlook Plaza Francia and Plaza Mitre (between Aguero and Pueyrredon), where the difference in levels has been taken advantage of to create one of the loveliest corners in Buenos Aires.

HOW TO GET THERE

Buses: Lines 17, 61, 62, 67, 92, 93, 101, 108, 110, 124.

The broken glass of the street lamp
should not discourage you from a twilight walk
through this enchanting zone of Buenos Aires.

Tour 7

As the porteños will have it, the word Palermo has more than
one meaning. From the census point of view, it refers to a huge
district of more than 1,000 blocks, whose limits run from the
river up to Cordoba St. on the east-west axis, while on the northern side it stretches as far as Belgrano and to Recoleta towards
the south.

On the other hand, whenever a porteño says that he is going
to Palermo, he absolutely means to visit a zone of gardens,
woods and lakes known as the largest and most important green
lung of the city.

There is also **Palermo Chico**, or Little Palermo. Its circu-
lar avenues and spider webb layout, splendid mansions many
of which embassies, make this exclusive corner of the city something really special. Situated on both sides of Fig. Alcorta Ave.,
between Tagle and San Martín de Tours streets, Palermo Chico is, along with Recoleta, one of the two most luxurious
residential areas in Buenos Aires.

Quite another thing is **Palermo Viejo** (old Palermo), actually the oldest quearter in the Palermo area. Honduras, Ser-
rano, Costa Rica, Guatemala, Plaza Guemes, are just a few of
its most typical haunts, where those traditional sausage houses
can still be seen. Formerly a tough neighborhood of bullies and
show-offs, Palermo Viejo in our days has become the bastion
of psychoanalists, and no wonder therefore if the dwellers have
been given to calling it Villa Freud.

Of all these Palermos, we have chosen touring the park, one
of the landmarks in B.A. that shouldn't be missed.

How it was

When a certain Juan Dominguez Palermo dared to make real estate investments in a zone that was only a lowland, with no decent roads and constantly outwashed by the river, Palermo started to become a neighborhood.

In 1836, Juan Manuel de Rosas took the lead and bought 540 blocks, thus turning into the owner of practically the whole area. Rosas built there his residence, where prominent foreign visitors as well as the porteño high society would gather. The mansion was located approximately where Libertador and Sarmiento avenues are today, but we must regret that it no longer exists and cannot appreciate its fine architectural lines.

The most important urban project though, was the filling of the land and the construction of drainage systems that changed this swampy area into what today is Parque Tres de Febrero (February 3rd Park). The choice of this name was no coincidence; February 3 is the date when Rosas was defeated in the Caseros battle by Urquiza's troops and it was only logical that this area be named after the historical event.

Anyhow, it would take 20 years for the project to turn the property into a public park come true. It was Sarmiento's idea, while Nicolas Avellaneda pushed the project forward, till on November 11, 1875, the porteños were able to see the official inauguration of the long awaited park.

How it is

The park in itself has not changed much, but we can't say the same with regard to the surroundings, where a complete network of avenues, plazas and roads gave much easier access to the zone, both to man and vehicles.

Plaza Italia — Your Palermo tour should start at Plaza Italia, where three important avenues meet: Las Heras, Santa Fe and Sarmiento. This small oval shaped plaza was never a dump, as most of the public parks in the old B.A. were. Everybody called it Plazoleta de los Portones (Gateway Plaza), on account of the large gates that marked the entrance to the Tres de Febrero Park. In 1904, the monument to Garibaldi was erected and so the place was called Plaza Italia. With the construction of the Zoo, the Botanical Gardens and the Rural Society,

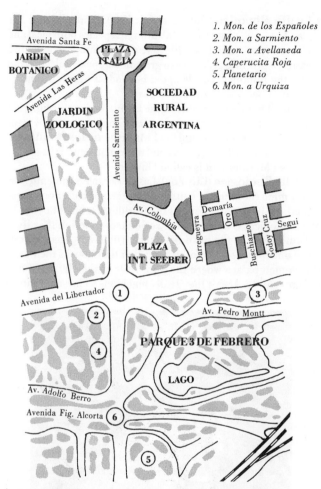

1. *Mon. de los Españoles*
2. *Mon. a Sarmiento*
3. *Mon. a Avellaneda*
4. *Caperucita Roja*
5. *Planetario*
6. *Mon. a Urquiza*

but specially when it became terminal for the first electric tramway, Plaza Italia grew in importance, till it became the hectic and heavily trafficked area we can see nowadays.

• **Sociedad Rural Argentina** (Argentine Rural Society); Santa Fe and Sarmiento Ave. — This is where the yearly cattle and agricultural show takes place.

If you are a breeder you surely have heard about it or have been here in the months when this expo takes place. If you are not, you can visit the Rural Society all year round, since the most disparate shows are held, all of great popular appeal.

• **Jardin Botanico** (Botanical Gardens); Santa Fe and Las Heras Ave. — With nearly 7,000 different species both local and acclimated, a specialized library, a gardening school, two theatres, a precious art nouveau greenhouse, peaceful lanes and paths, the Botanical Garden goes beyond its purely scientific interest to become a real urban oasis.

Carlos Thays, responsible of the layout, chose a design that reproduces the regions where the plants come from. A few steps from the entrance you'll find the **Estanque de los Nenúfares** (Nympheas' Pond), with a beautiful nude in its center; its author is Correa Morales and is called Ondine.

• **Jardin Zoologico** (City Zoo); Las Heras and Sarmiento Ave. Never mind the animals, neither different, nor better nor worse than those in any other zoo of the world; what must be seen in our Zoological Garden are the residences in which they live.

Don't smile at the word residence, you might change your mind once you see the gothic pavillion that houses the bears, the French palace where the lions live, or the elefants Bombayian temple. Aren't they really mansions? The same can be

Zoological Gardens
With cages like this one, we don't really know what
the public admires most: the housing or its inhabitants.

said about the buffalos Indostan temple or the condors' Eiffel Tower shaped cage.

The zoo, in fact, is a lovely nonsense, but also a didactical corner where everything seems to fit in its place. There are quality sculptures, some of which copies, as **Niña con Flores** (A Girl with Flowers) by Antonio Canova, or the **Templo de Vesta** (Temple of Vesta) which you'll see on entering the grounds. But others are original, like the **Bizantine Ruins**, a seven-column portico rising at the rear of the Darwin Lake (at the entrance). So perfect is the deterioration that it would seem the whole thing is a fake; instead, they are authentic columns brought from Trieste, where they used to adorn a Bizantine palace and now rest in a "remote" corner of the world known as Buenos Aires.

Before leaving the zoo, check your time —if you'are able to— in the sun clock incorporated to a nude near the Av. Libertador gate. Just as the tradition demands of this type of clocks, an inscription will assure you that "it only marks the happy hours". Of course, it tells you so in Latin.

The Zoo - Byzantine Ruins.
This authentic byzantine colonnade was brought
from Venice to the River Plate.
It is enjoyed both by porteños and flamingos.

Monumento de los españoles (The Spaniards Monument); Sarmiento and Libertador Ave. — On leaving the Zoo through the Av. Libertador gate, you'll come face to face with an imposing marble monument called, God knows why, "Magna Carta and the Four Argentine Regions".

Don't try to keep in mind such a complicated name for just a simple idea: the fraternity of Spaniards and Argentines ow-

The Spaniards Monument.

ing to idiomatic and racial ties. The monument was actually a gift from the Spanish people on the 100th anniversary of our independence and from that very moment it became for everybody The Spaniards' Monument.

The name is obviously nothing to write home about, but the monument is really wonderful. Made by the catalonian sculptor Agustín Querol, this immaculate white marble structure towers 25 meters high, with the figure of the Republic on the top, her vestments blowing in the wind. On two sides of the base, large pools collect the sprouting water and in each of the corners are the allegories of the aforesaid regions: the Andes, the River Plate, Chaco and La Pampa. They are four bronze figures cut in the neoclassic style, while at the base of the pedestal and climbing around it, the carving turns to a modernist style, the name that art nouveau acquired in Spain.

This monument is surely among the best we have in B.A. and its privileged location enables you to appreciate it clearly outlined against the sky. Even on cloudy days it looks gorgeous.

Parque Tres de Febrero/Bosques de Palermo

(February 3rd. Park/Palermo Woods) — Finally, we have reached the heart of Palermo: the park, which occupies 291 hectares full of gardens, lakes and woods surrounded by Av. Libertador, Salguero, the Riverside Drive and Pampa.

Palermo holds some resemblance with the parisian Bois de Boulogne, which is no wonder at all since the person responsible for the final outline of our park and the remodelling of the Bois was the same: Carlos Thays. Thays was director of the Public Parks Office and while he was in charge the city acquired an enormous quantity of trees that transformed a flat and melancholy town into a metropolis full of color and beauty.

But, next to its trees and lakes, Palermo can also boast many pieces of sculpture. This is another very typical feature of Buenos Aires, one of the cities in the world with the greatest number of statues along streets and plazas, even in far away districts.

• **Monumento a Sarmiento** (Sarmiento Monument), by Auguste Rodin (in front of the Spaniards Monument). There were times in B.A. when the urge for progress wanted the best for the best, and the Argentine government didn't hesitate to commission the renowned French sculptor the task of perpetuating the memory of a man who had done so much to improve culture in the country.

Rodin accomplished a simple composition, made of a marble base on which the bronze statue of Sarmiento stands. There is vigor and dinamism in this figure, carried out by the artist in a style very similar to that of his famous Balzac.

On the rear face of the pedestal a carving of our national emblem can be seen, although as a matter of fact it doesn't exactly follow the real shape of the symbol.

Behind the monument, which occupies the site where Rosas had his residence, you'll see a sprout of the so called **Aromo del Perdon** (The Myrth of Mercy), under whose shade Manuelita, the daughter of Rosas, would obtain from her father mercy for the political prisoners who appealed to her in search of help.

• **Caperucita Roja** (Little Red Riding Hood). In this same sector of the park but closer to Av. Fig. Alcorta you'll come across with this sculpture that will surely arise your attention. As far as we know, the heroine of the most famous tale of all times has only one statue in the world and it is standing in Palermo. From her original setting in the district of Belgrano, Little Red Riding Hood moved to Plaza Lavalle and then to Palermo, where she seems at last happily settled and certainly not unnoticed.

• **Monumento a Avellaneda** (Monument to Avellaneda), by Jose Fioravanti; Av. del Libertador and Godoy Cruz. An imposing piece of sculpture indeed, with three clearly outlined sectors: a pedestal, a middle area with statues and reliefs, and a crowning with the figure of Avellaneda, although the latter is not the most appealing feature of the monument but the seating statue which appears in the center.

Fioravanti's style is obviously influenced by Egyptian sculpture, which results in grandiose figures of powerful impact on the viewer.

This monument must be observed taking different angles so as to appreciated every sector of the composition, mainly when the sun rays enhance its volume.

Planetario (Planetarium); Av. Sarmiento and Belisario Roldan.

Besides your artistic tour, take a bit of time off and visit the Galileo Galilei Planetarium, a "star" not to be missed. As a matter of fact, the stars here are some 9,000, along with the sun, the moon and the planets, magnificently reproduced on the large dome of the projection hall. Conferences are also held here, which usually prove to be appealing to the young and the

old. Admission to the Planetarium is not allowed to children under seven since the show might be tiresome for them. And you
certainly know what a bored kid means... *Saturdays and Sundays 4:30, 6 and 7:30.*

*Monument to Sarmiento, by Rodin.
The statue is rather small, but the moral value
of Sarmiento was great.*

Los mateos (The coaches) — Though the expanse of the
Parque 3 de Febrero and the surrounding woods is considerable, you should do your touring on foot. Now, if you are looking for a fascinating experience, a mateo ride is your choice.
The mateo is a kind of typical horse driven coach, whose name
dates back to 1924 after a popular play by Argentine writer Ar-
mando Discepolo in which the protagonist, a driver himself of

one of these cabbies, was actually called Mateo.

Palermo is nowadays the last corner in Buenos Aires where these true relics of the past can still be seen. A ride on board of one of them, plus a good deal of romanticism, will let your imagination fly either to the luxuries of the good old times or to the benefits of our speedy age.

COSTANERA NORTE

Your Palermo tour won't be complete without a visit to the North riverside. You can get there through Av. Sarmiento or, better still, down Salguero St., where the Palermo area begins.

And here, at the North Riverside, you'll finally be able to see the river. But not the opposite shore. The so called "widest river in the world" will prove true when no matter how much you strain your eyes you'll hardly make out the thin hazy line of the Uruguayan coast, unless it is a perfectly clear day.

Anyhow, the Costanera has a lot to offer. If it is summertime, the possibility to bask away in the sun on some little beach; bathing is still not allowed, since the waters are poluted in all the Capital's waterfront. By the way the brownish colored water is due to the lime at its bottom, and not because it is disgustingly dirty, as some ill minded people would like us to believe.

If you are fond of fishing, you can indulge to it all along the riverside drive and you can also take advantage of the **Club de Pescadores** (Fishermen's Club). But even if fishing is not your game, take a minute to visit this club, a beautiful example of good architecture.

Just in front of the Fishermen's Club you'll find the **Aeroparque Metropolitano** (Metropolitan Airport), terminal to all domestic and regional flights. The Airport is perfectly integrated to its surroundings and is the chosen place for many porteños in their sunday outings.

While you are there, it is more than worthwhile to visit the **Museo Nacional Aeronautico** (National Aeronautical Museum), located at 4550 Rafael Obligado Ave. (that is to say, the riverside drive). In this museum you'll be able to see interesting testimonies of man's ancestral desire to fly, from mythological Icarus right up to the most advanced technologies, without forgetting the ever modern Leonardo Da Vinci. *Thursdays 1 to 4 pm. Saturdays and Sundays 1 to 5 pm.*

The Planetarium.
A fine way to visit the galaxies from a restful amchair.

WHERE TO EAT IN THIS AREA

HOSTAL DEL LAGO - Fig. Alcorta 6100 (Palermo Woods)
MAMMA LEONE - Canning 3624
THE HORSE - Av. Libertador y Av. Bullrich
BISTRO - Demaria y Sinclair
"CARRITOS" - Costanera Norte
CERVECERIA PALERMO TENIS - Demaria 4721
DEMARIA - Demaria 4722
EL OSO CHARLY'S - Juan F. Segui 4676
EL REFUGIO DEL VIEJO CONDE - Cerviño 4453
LE COIN - Sinclair 3102
MAISON FROMAGE - Demaria 4672
PAPARAZZI - Juan F. Segui 4690
PARRILLA "RIO ALBA" - Cerviño 4499
PUERTO MARISKO - Demaria 4658

North Riverside
A paradise for romantic folk and patient fishermen.
Sometimes they get together.

The River Plate.
B.A. has turned its back on it, but porteños
always keep it dep in their heart.

Los Carritos (The Dinners) — One of the main reasons to go down to the north riverside are the Carritos. And what is that? Well, they are the equivalent to american dinners. Surely you have already seen them all along the drive, except for the area taken up by the Airport.

Nowadays they barely look like a dinner, but not long ago they were really trailers, small carts which had been turned into barbacue stands for night fishermen and earlybird truck drivers. The job over, the fire was put out, the make-shift wooden or zinc counter packed away, and the dinner would drive off until the next day.

The excellence of the meat offered at these unusual eateries became vox populi and many of these cheap drivein barbacues flourished. The great amount of public led to the improvement of the installations and so the picturesque had to give way to hygiene and comfort. The old dinners became conventional but luxurious restaurants with definitely unconventional names, and the menu, besides the ever present barbacue, included the most sophisticated dishes of the international cuisine.

Still there are the wide river, the caress of the winter sun through large glass windows, or the fresh summer breeze on terraces and gardens. Hurry up, then, and run to the carritos! You'll like them.

HOW TO GET THERE

Subway: Line D - PLAZA ITALIA station.

Buses: Lines 12, 29, 36, 37, 38, 39, 41, 55, 59, 60, 64, 67, 68, 93, 95, 111, 118, 130, 141, 152.

If you have time...

...don't miss the outskirts of Buenos Aires, where you'll find places of great beauty and interest, among which we have selected the most important and nearest to the city. In all cases they are easily reached by train or bus.

LA PLATA

When Buenos Aires was federalized, in 1880, a place was needed for the provincial authorities and two years later the city of La Plata was founded. It was designed by Pedro Benoit jr (son of the co-author of the Metropolitan Cathedral's portico), who made a geometrical layout, abundant in diagonal avenues and green spaces, both very typical features of this beautiful city situated 50 km south from Buenos Aires.

The center of La Plata is Plaza Mariano Moreno, which includes the Town Hall and the **Cathedral**. The latter is certainly one of the most outstanding landmarks in the city, an imposing building fit for 14,000 people that combines a mixture of medieval styles and stands as a clear example of last century architectural eclecticism in Argentina. Noteworthy are the stained glass windows, an exact replica of those in Chartres and actually supervised by French experts. We suggest you visit the Cathedral no later than 2 or 3 pm, so as to be able to enjoy light effects at their best.

Other important buildings in La Plata are the Government Palace and the Legislature, both on Plaza San Martin, as well as the Dardo Rocha Center and the Law Courts.

But the highlight in La Plata is undoubtedly the **Paseo del Bosque** (Forest Promenade), a huge park in which you'll find the Martin Fierro Theatre, the Astronomical Observatory, a Zoo and the world famous **Museo de Ciencias Naturales** (Natural Sciences Museum) which makes on its own the visit to La Plata a must. Its collections of perfectly reconstructed prehistoric animals are certainly one of its main attractions, although also interesting are the Archaeological halls and especially that of Anthropology, exhibiting skeletons and skulls belonging to the Jibaros, a Peruvian Indian tribe well known because of their macabre skill to shrink heads. *Every day except National holidays, from 1 to 6 pm.*

How to get there: Train from Constitucion Station. Bus: Rio de la Plata Line, leaving from Retiro, Constitucion, or Plaza Once Stations.

ISLANDS OF TIGRE

You really can't miss this place, situated but 32 km north of B.A. and a 40 minutes train ride.

Just before reaching its mouth in the River Plate, the Parana, a rapid flowing river that comes from the north, opens up into a huge delta of nearly 14,000 km² criss-crossed by rivers, rivulets and streams forming an uncountable amount of islands.

Forests of willows and poplers, thick rushes along the shore lines, hydrangeas and other plants teeming with flowers, around luxurious weekend houses as well as simple wood shaks on pilons, make up a gorgeous scenery unique in the world.

The key to the Delta is the small city of Tigre, where you'll find the docks. There are two hour tours up to all day visits, with places reserved for camping and many inns and hotels to spend the night. All needed information is available on the pier.

If you are not fond of sailing, you can choose to tour the residential area of Tigre, which you'll enter after crossing the bridge at the head of the station. On **Paseo Victorica** (the riverside avenue) plenty of restaurants, cafes and nautical clubs are found standing amidst the chalets.

El Tigre (The Tiger), as this place is popularly known, used to be the élite's tourist center at the turn of the century and in its time could boast the country's first casino. The treasured Tigre Club has been turned into a cultural center but the building, an opulent palace nowadays known as **Tigre Hotel**, fortunately still keeps some of its splendor of old.

The Tigre islands are attractive at any time of the year, vegetation is always exuberant, permanent dwellers enliven the surroundings, and the waters are never lacking in rowing boats and vessels of all types, from canoes to luxury yachts. And in Spring, the perfume of the ligustrum in bloom is what you'd call inebriant.

How to get there: By train, from Retiro Station (Mitre Line) or by Bus # 60, which goes as far as the Tigre Hotel. If you can manage to travel by car, you'll be able to make brief stopovers at the beautiful coastal districts of Olivos, Martinez, San Isidro, etc., thus getting the most out of the visit.

LUJAN

Located 71 km west of B.A., Lujan is one of the most important tourist and pilgrimage centers in the country.

The city was born and grew around its church, whose origin is quite picturesque. As far as the legend goes, a wagon carrying an image of the Virgin got stuck in the mud while crossing the river. No matter how hard the animals heaved, they would not make the wagon budge, and only when the figure was unloaded did it move. This was taken as a sign that the Virgin wished to remain in that place and then and there a rudimentary altar was erected which would become the imposing Basilica we can see nowadays.

The construction started in 1887, but only in 1935 was finished. The building is a noble gothic revival and deserves to be attentively appreciated, from its magnificent facade to its beautiful chapels and stained glass windows in the interior.

Lujan is also a historic city, witness to many important events. It was here that Viceroy Sobremonte took refuge when the British troops invaded B.A.; later, it became a prison camp for political dissidents.

Nowadays, many historical mementos are housed in the buildings of the **Complejo Museografico Enrique Udaondo** (Enrique Udaondo Museum Complex), divided in three sections.

The first is known as the **Museo Histórico y Colonial** (Historical and Colonial Museum) that holds the old Cabildo; next to it is the so called Viceroy's House. The Museum treasures over 30,000 pieces related to Argentine history. You'll probably find quite interesting the dungeons, where wax figures represent acts of torture popular at that time. This part of the museum also offers a fashion hall and another totally dedicated to the legendary gaucho Martin Fierro, that came to life through Jose Hernandez's book.

The **Museo del Transporte** (Transportation Museum)

makes up the second section, where more than 60 vehicles from various periods can be appreciated. You'll be able to see ancient carts dating back to colonial times, along with different presidential carriages and B.A.'s first tramway. But the star of the museum is *La Porteña*, the country's first train engine, that used to travel from Plaza Lavalle to the town of La Floresta.

The last sector is devoted to automobiles. Here you'll admire a collection of 23 cars, among which a 1887 Mercedes Benz, a 1892 Daimler, and the Argentina built 1927 Yuram.

In summer Lujan offers river front resorts and camping areas; sail and motor boats as well as leisure cruisers are available and horses can be hired, all of which providing a full day's outdoors entertainment.

How to get there: Train from Plaza Once or bus leaving from the same station (Automotores Lujan Co.).

We suggest you devote some of your time to visit the neighborhoods and suburbs of Buenos Aires. You will find there an utterly different city.

San Isidro.
A corner of the port, where smaller sized vessels anchor.

Are you planning to leave without doing any shopping?

Of course not. Whether you openly admit it or not, it is a fact that to go shopping is one of the most fascinating things about travelling abroad.

Florida St. and Santa Fe Ave. are the largest and favorite shopping areas. On these two streets and their surrounding ones, you can find absolutely everything, in all qualities and for any budget.

Haute Couture has its own district in Barrio Norte and Recoleta. The most refined garments can be found along Arenales, Juncal, Quintana, Alvear and Callao Avenues.

If books is what you are looking for, Corrientes is the place, just as you'll find the heart of record shops along Lavalle St.

Shopping galleries, that make the treasure hunt ever so easier, are abundant in Buenos Aires. An interesting spot is Galeria del Este, on Florida at the 900 block. In the sixties it used to be a hippy corner full of shops with unusual items and clothing; nowadays those exotic places have turned into top quality stores.

Are you looking for bargains? You can find them anywhere if you have the time to look around, especially when sales come around and prices go down between 30 and 40 per cent.

Now, to really buy cheaply, there is no place like Once, an almost exclusive garment district on the streets surrounding Corrientes Ave. and Azcuenaga St. But even if prices are not always that low, it is all the same a curious quarter which can help you to get acquainted with the multiple faces of the city.

Evidently, porteños adore shopping, and you'll notice that most of B.A.'s stores have their windows decorated with exquisite good taste, of course only to encourage our devotion to spend. That is why any selection of addresses we could offer to you would always be a personal and hence, arbitrary choice.

Because, believe us: you don't need any advice to spend money in Buenos Aires!

Buenos Aires sights

(Listed alphabetically)

MONUMENTS AND STATUES

MUSEUMS

PARKS AND SQUARES

STREETS AND AVENUES

THEATRES

MISCELLANEA

Se terminó de imprimir
en los talleres de IMPRECO GRÁFICA
Viel 1448, Buenos Aires,
en el mes de junio de 1996.